MW01015731

Savoring Sandpoint

Recipes Across the Long Bridge

Community Assistance League
PO Box 1361
Sandpoint, ID 83864
208.263.3400

Editor
Diana M. Carlson

Food & Recipe Editors
Barbara Balbi, Betsy Harding, Shawna Parry & Barbara Wilcox

Design Team
Laura Bry, Foster Cline, MD., Sally Park

Cookbook Committees

Chairman
Valerie Albi

Advisory Board
Mindy Cameron
Tracy Gibson
Charie Kerr
Charlene Krames
Sally Lowry
Maribeth Lynch
Lynn Piper
Jane Riter
Judy Thompson
Marcia Wilson
Carol Whittom
Sue Vogelsinger

Committee Chairmen
Helen Williams-Baker
Hermie Cline
Betty Ann Diehl
Barbara Eacret
Heather Hellier
Sally Lindemann
Sue Malletta
Sherry Metz
Patricia Otto
Carol Page
Ann Roen
Pat Ramsey
Darlene Shelly
Jeanelle Shields

First Edition
© 2006. All rights reserved.
Community Assistance League
PO Box 1361
Sandpoint, ID 83864
208.263.3400

The cookbook is a collection of favorite recipes tested in the kitchens of great cooks. The recipes may not be original.

Contents

Ardis Racicot, circa early 1900s
Robert Gunter Collection

Introduction

Traditionally the American woman found her publishing voice by writing cookbooks. There was an instant audience, a mutual bond, and a way to link food, family and traditions.

Savoring Sandpoint-Recipes Across the Long Bridge has a blend of recipes from the kitchens of great cooks. Our cookbook blends Sandpoint's beauty along with some of our favorite historical scenes. We celebrate serving our community.

Community Assistance League

Dorothy Culver near today's Jeff Jones Memorial Park.
Notice Bellwood Furniture on right, circa 1920s.
Bonner County Historical Society Collection

August Long Bridge Swim, Sandpoint
Foster Cline, MD.

Appetizers

Savoring Sandpoint's past at a Garden Party in the back yard at Inatz Weil's Home in the early 1900s. Home of the late

L. D. and Gertrude McFarland. McFarland's back yard, First Avenue, Sandpoint, Idaho. Bonner County Historical Society

Black Bean Torte
Serves eight to ten

2	cups dried black beans
2	14 oz. cans chicken broth
1	boullion cube
2	cups water
1	tsp. ground cumin
1	large tomato, seeded and chopped with excess juice pressed out
½	cup thinly chopped red onion
4	ozs. crumbled feta cheese
½	cup sour cream
	cilantro leaves for garnish

Cilantro Pesto

2	bunches fresh cilantro leaves
2	tbsp. olive oil
1	tsp. pressed garlic
½	cup pine nuts

1. Place rinsed black beans in large pan. Add chicken broth, bouillon cube, water and cumin. Bring to boil. Cover and simmer approximately 2½ hours until beans are tender. Stir mixture occasionally. Mash 1 cup of beans. Gently hand mix remaining whole beans with mashed beans. Cool.

2. Pureé cilantro pesto ingredients in food processor or blender.

3. Line 4" x 8" loaf pan with plastic wrap with edges

overlapping rim. Gently press ⅓ bean mixture into pan, making layer smooth. Spread cilantro pesto over bean mixture.

4. Press another ⅓ of bean mixture over cilantro pesto, making the bean layer smooth.

5. On top of beans, make an even layer of chopped tomatoes and onions. Sprinkle feta cheese on top of the mixture.

6. Top cheese with remaining beans, pressing gently to make a smooth loaf. Cover tightly with plastic wrap and refrigerate until loaf is firm.

7. Invert loaf onto platter and remove plastic wrap. Spoon sour cream down center and garnish with cilantro leaves.

Serve with crackers or tortilla chips, or slice into ½" pieces and serve as a first course.

Brie with Fruit & Nuts

1   8" round Brie cheese

Mince up the following:

1   pear
1   Granny Smith Apple
1   cup pecans coarsely chopped
1   cup yellow raisins
½   cup dried apricots
½   cup dried dates
1   cup apple cider
      brown sugar to taste

1. Mince fruit and mix in bowl.

2. Add brown sugar to taste. Pour in enough apple cider to cover mixture.

3. Marinate overnight.

4. Spread mixture on top of Brie.

5. Preheat oven to 350°. Bake until Brie melts (about 15 minutes).

Chili Cheese Appetizers

½   cup butter
10   eggs
½   cup flour
       dash salt
1   pint cottage cheese
1   lb. jack cheese, shredded (Can use ½ Cheddar and ½ jack cheese)
1   tsp. baking powder
1   8 oz. can green chili peppers, chopped

Preheat oven to 400°.

1. Melt butter in 13" x 9" pan.

2. Beat eggs slightly with a fork and fold in rest of ingredients.

3. Bake for 35 to 40 minutes.

4. Cut into wedges and serve for an appetizer, breakfast or lunch.

Can prepare this ahead of time and reheat. May be baked and frozen.

Nancy Bell Wray born in Kentucky 1872. Taught in Sandpoint 1897. Married Earl Farmin 1900.

Chutney Cheese Ball

2   oz. cream cheese, softened
1   cup sharp cheddar cheese, grated
¼   cup sherry
¼   tsp. curry powder
3   green onions and tops, finely sliced
1   cup chutney

1. Mix cheeses, sherry and curry powder well.

2. Shape into a ball and chill overnight to blend flavors.

3. Place on serving plate; top with chutney. Sprinkle green onions over top.

4. Serve with crackers.

This is an easy, make-ahead appetizer. Use Major Gray's Chutney and let it dribble down the sides.

Gorgonzola Cocktail Tarts
Makes three dozen

3	large eggs
½	tsp. chopped fresh rosemary
1½	cups low-fat cottage cheese
¼	cup melted butter
½	cup crumbled blue cheese or Gorgonzola (packed)
3	tbsp. sour cream
½	tsp. salt
¼	tsp. black pepper
	walnut or pecan halves, or pine nuts

Preheat oven to 400°.

1. Spray 36 mini-muffin cups with nonstick spray.

2. In large bowl, whisk eggs with next 7 ingredients to blend well.

3. Fill each cup with a generous tablespoon of batter. Top each cup with half a nut if using walnuts or pecans, or several pine nuts.

4. Bake tarts until golden and puffed, about 28 minutes. Cool for 5 minutes in pans before removing.

5. Serve warm from oven or at room temperature.

If making ahead, cool tarts completely in pans after baking. Wrap in foil and refrigerate. To serve, reheat uncovered at 350° for 10 minutes.

Greek Pâté
Makes two dozen

2	tbsp. coarsely chopped fresh basil
3	tbsp. julienne sun-dried tomatoes
3	tbsp. crumbled feta cheese
8	oz. softened cream cheese

1. Wash basil and pat dry. Chop coarsely. Blot oil from sun-dried tomatoes and julienne. (Reserve a few slices for garnish.)

2. Combine all ingredients and press firmly into a one-cup decorative bowl. Decorate with small basil leaves and strips of tomato.

3. Serve on whole-grain crackers or pita bread cut into triangles.

Greek Style Spinach Tarts

Serves six

6	frozen patty shells, thawed
½	cup chopped onion
1	tbsp. oil
1	10 oz. pkg. frozen, chopped spinach, thawed and drained
1	cup crumbled feta cheese
1	cup cottage cheese
1	beaten egg
¼	tsp. salt
¼	tsp. pepper

Preheat oven to 400°.

1. Roll out each patty shell between sheets of waxed paper to form a 7½" circle. Chill.

2. Sauté onion in oil until tender. Add spinach; cook, stirring until all liquid evaporates. Cool. Stir in cheeses, egg, salt, and pepper.

3. Take one shell at a time from refrigerator and carefully remove waxed paper (if pastry sticks, place in freezer a few minutes). Place ½ cup spinach mixture in center of pastry. Fold over to form semicircle. Fold edges over and press well to seal. Carefully transfer to ungreased cookie sheet.

4. Bake for 30 to 35 minutes, or until pastry is golden brown.

Green Chile Cheese Puffs

Makes two dozen

½	cup butter, room temperature
2	cups grated aged Cheddar cheese
½	tsp. dry mustard
½	tsp. seasoned salt
2	tsp. finely chopped canned green chilies
2	tsp. finely chopped pimiento
½	tsp. Worcestershire sauce
1¼	cups sifted all-purpose flour

Preheat oven to 350°.

1. Beat until blended: butter, cheese, mustard, salt, chilies, pimiento and Worcestershire sauce. Add flour, a little at a time and mix until dough is stiff.

2. Form small balls of dough and place on a cookie sheet.

3. Bake for 15 to 20 minutes or until lightly brown.

Serve warm or cold as appetizers or snacks.

Hummus

2	tbsp. sesame seeds
1	15 ½ oz. can garbanzo beans, rinsed and drained
3	tbsp. lemon juice
2	tbsp olive oil
2	tbsp. non-fat yogurt or non-fat sour cream
1	tbsp. fresh parsley, minced
1	tbsp. fresh mint, minced
2	tbsp. sesame tahini
½	tsp. cumin
2	cloves fresh garlic
½	tsp. cayenne pepper
¼	tsp. salt

1. In frying pan, over medium heat, toast sesame seeds until golden, about 5 minutes. Set aside to cool.

2. Combine remaining ingredients in blender or food processor and blend until mixture is smooth. Add sesame seeds and set aside to "cure" about 1 hour.

3. Spoon into serving bowl and drizzle with olive oil. Serve with crackers or pita bread pieces. Can also be used as sandwich spread.

Leek and Feta Cheese

Serves six

2	tbsp.olive oil
1	tsp. chopped fresh rosemary
3	cloves garlic, minced
1	leek, chopped coarsely
½	lb. mushrooms, chopped coarsely
1	tomato, chopped coarsely
¼	lb. feta cheese, crumbled
¼	lb. provolone cheese, ½ cubed, ½ sliced
¼	cup sherry
	salt and pepper to taste

Preheat oven to 325°.

1. Sauté rosemary, garlic, leek and mushrooms in olive oil; add tomato, sherry, salt and pepper.

2. While mixture is still warm, stir in feta and cubed provolone cheese.

3. Spread mixture in a shallow 1 quart dish.

4. Cover with sliced provolone and bake for about 20 minutes. Then broil until it bubbles.

Serve with crusty bread. Good as side dish or appetizer. Can make ahead, refrigerate and bake before serving.

Mango Salsa

3	mangos, chopped
1	tart apple, chopped
⅓	juice of one lemon or lime
½	red onion, diced
½	red pepper, chopped
½	bunch cilantro, chopped
2	tsp. ground cumin
½	tsp. ground ginger
4	tbsp. brown sugar

1. Toss the apple pieces with lemon or lime juice.

2. Combine all ingredients in a bowl.

This is a great side dish with chicken or fish; also try with taco chips.

Nineteen year-old Ruthe Caroline Smith Bond photographed
on the Sandpoint Bridge, 1918. Her mom thought Ruthe's
new $7.00 hat was extravagant. Ruthe worked as a
proofreader at the local paper

Carol Bond Bowie and Diana Bond Collection

Marjoram Dip

Serves six to eight

1½	cups sour cream
¼	cup softened cream cheese
¼	cup finely chopped shallots
2	tbsp. chopped chives
1-2	tbsp. finely chopped fresh marjoram
½	tsp. dried marjoram
1¼	tsp. coarsely ground tri-colored pepper
½	tsp. coarse kosher salt
	additional chives, marjoram and pepper for garnish

1. Mix sour cream and softened cream cheese until smooth.

2. Add remaining ingredients and blend in food processor.

3. Chill overnight.

4. Garnish with additional fresh chopped marjoram, chives and tri-colored pepper. Serve with crackers, veggies or chips.

May Wine
Serves eight to ten

12-20   sweet woodruff sprigs

3   pints fresh ripe strawberries (reserve one pint for garnish)

2   bottles of slightly sweet white wine (Rhine wine works well)

½   cup sugar

1   bottle of champagne

Garnish

Use any of the following: woodruff sprigs and their blossoms; violets, Johnny-jumps, pansies, rose petals, or other edible flower blossoms.

Preheat oven to 200°.

1. Heat 12 to 20 woodruff sprigs on a baking sheet until fragrant, about 5 minutes.

2. Remove stems from 2 pints of strawberries.

3. Add a pint of strawberries to each of 2 pitchers along with ½ cup of sugar if berries are too tart, or less if they are sweet. Crush berries with the sugar. Divide woodruff evenly between the two pitchers.

4. Pour a bottle of wine into each pitcher; stir well, and refrigerate overnight or up to 24 hours.

5. Before serving strain wine into punch bowl. Add an ice mold and a bottle of champagne. Garnish with reserved strawberries, woodruff and edible flowers.

Ruth Steen and son, June 3, 1914
Robert Gunter Collection

Olivita Crostini
Serves six to eight

5	oz. chopped black or Kalamata olives
½	cup finely chopped pimiento stuffed green olives
½	cup grated Parmesan cheese
4	tbsp. unsalted butter at room temperature
1	tsp. extra-virgin olive oil
2	cloves garlic, minced
¾	cup shredded Monterey Jack cheese
¼	cup minced fresh Italian parsley
1	crusty French baguette

Preheat broiler

1. In medium bowl, stir together olives, Parmesan, butter, oil and garlic until well blended. Stir in Monterey Jack and parsley.

2. Cut baguette into 25 thin slices. Arrange bread slices on baking sheets and spread olive mixture on each.

3. Broil 3 to 4 minutes or until bread is toasted at edges and Olivita is bubbly.

Original Swiss Fondue
Serves four to six

1	loaf sourdough bread
1	lb. Emmentaler cheese
1	lb. Gruyere cheese
2-3	tbsp. all-purpose flour
4	garlic cloves, freshly peeled
4	tbsp. unsalted butter
2	cups dry white wine
½	lemon
1	oz. Kirsch, brandy or sherry

Preheat oven to 350°.

1. Cut Emmentaler and Gruyere cheeses into ¼" cubes and lightly flour.

2. Cut bread into 1" cubes and brown in oven for about 15 minutes.

3. Heat butter in large heavy sauce pan. Very lightly brown garlic over low heat. Remove garlic.

4. Slowly add all white wine (Wine boils at 175 °; do not let it boil). Begin adding cheese when wine is at least 140°. Do not add more than about 20% of cheese at a time. Stir in a figure 8 pattern, so that most of cheese melts before adding more.

5. After all cheese is melted, add juice of ½ lemon and the Kirsch.

6. Serve in fondue pot with a warmer. Dip toasted bread cubes into cheese and enjoy!

Pizza Popcorn

½   cup melted butter
1   pkg. dry spaghetti seasoning or
     Italian seasoning
2   pinches oregano

Mix and toss over large bowl of popped popcorn.

Orange Shrimp Appetizer
Serves eight to ten

⅓	cup olive oil
5	tbsp. sherry wine vinegar
1	garlic clove, pressed
2	tsp. sugar
1	tbsp. grated orange peel
2	tbsp. minced onion
2	tbsp. capers
1	tbsp. chopped parsley
1	lb. shelled, cooked shrimp (medium to large)
1	cup large olives, black or green
	lettuce leaves, paprika, orange slices

1. Whisk together first 5 ingredients. Add onions, capers and parsley.

2. Pour marinade over shrimp and olives. Let stand at room temperature for at least 30 minutes.

3. In dish lined with crisp lettuce leaves, mound shrimp and olives. Garnish with orange slices and sprinkle with paprika.

Offer with party picks, or serve with a hearty bread to dip in the marinade.

Salmon Party Pinwheels

Makes 40 appetizers

1	7¼ oz. can red salmon, or 8 oz. smoked salmon
¾	cup shredded Cheddar cheese
2	tbsp. finely chopped green onion
3	tbsp. finely chopped pimiento-stuffed olives
¼	tsp. dill weed
¼	tsp. pepper or to taste
2	tsp. fresh lemon juice
¼	cup mayonnaise
1	8 oz. package refrigerated crescent rolls

Preheat oven to 375°.

1. Flake salmon and combine with all ingredients, except dough.

2. Divide dough into 4 rectangles, pinching seams together.

3. Spread ¼ of salmon filling on each rectangle. Roll up from the long sides. Cut each into 10 pinwheels.

4. Place cut sides down on greased baking sheet.

5. Bake for 12 to 15 minutes or until golden.

Shrimp and Artichoke Hearts

1   lb. medium, cooked, ready to eat shrimp
1   14-oz can artichoke hearts (in water) drained
½   small onion, sliced into rings
½   cup sliced water chestnuts

Marinade
½   cup olive oil
¼   cup seasoned rice vinegar
2   tsp. fresh parsley
½   tsp. sugar
¼   tsp. salt
¼   tsp. paprika
¼   tsp. whole black peppercorns
½   garlic clove, minced

1. Combine marinade ingredients in large jar; cover and shake well.

2. In large bowl, combine shrimp, artichoke-hearts, onion slices and water chestnuts.

3. Pour marinade over shrimp/artichoke mixture. Cover and refrigerate overnight.

Serve with crackers or provide toothpicks for spearing, or drain and serve on silver tray lined with parsley or curly lettuce.

Jeannie Whitaker, circa 1910
Robert Gunter Collection

Spanish Frittata

Serves eight

½   lb. cheese-onion or cheese-jalapeño bread, cut into ½" cubes
½   cup chopped onion
2   tbsp. olive oil
9   large eggs
2   cups milk
1   cup (4 oz.) shredded jack cheese
1   cup(4 oz.) shredded Cheddar cheese
1   7 oz. can diced green chilies
¼   cup chopped fresh Anaheim chilies
¼   cup chopped fresh cilantro
2   tbsp. chopped fresh parsley
1   tsp. salt

Garnish

avocado slices
salsa
sour cream

1. Spread bread evenly in buttered 9" x 13" pan.

2. Sauté onion in oil.

3. In a bowl, beat eggs and milk just to blend. Add jack cheese, Cheddar cheese, canned chilies, sautéed onion, fresh chilies, chopped cilantro, parsley and salt. Pour evenly over bread.

4. Cover and chill at least eight hours or overnight.

5. Uncover and bake in a 350° oven until center barely jiggles when gently shaken and top is lightly browned, about 45 minutes.

6. Cut into pieces and serve with mild salsa, sour cream and avocado slices.

Spiced Nuts

1	cup butter
4	cups walnuts or pecans
3	cups powdered sugar
2	tbsp. cinnamon
2	tbsp. ground cloves
2	tbsp. ground nutmeg

1. Melt butter and add nuts. Stir over low heat about 20 minutes until nuts are lightly brown.

2. In paper bag, combine sugar and spices. Put in nuts and shake until generously coated.

3. Pour into colander to shake off excess sugar.

4. Spread nuts on paper towels to cool and dry.

Make these to give away as gifts.

Spicy Herb Roasted Nuts

1½	cups almonds
1½	cups walnut halves
1	cup filberts
1	cup pecan halves
½	cup real maple syrup
¼	tsp. cayenne pepper
¼	tsp. sage
¼	tsp. thyme
¼	tsp. marjoram
¼	tsp. rosemary
¼	tsp. savory
¼	tsp. oregano
3	tbsp. olive oil
1	tsp. kosher salt

Preheat oven to 300º.

1. Mix nuts, maple syrup, cayenne, herbs and oil in large bowl. Spread in rimmed pan lined with heavy duty aluminum foil. Sprinkle nuts with salt.

2. Bake about 45 minutes. Stir occasionally, until all liquid evaporates and almonds and filberts are golden under the skin. (Break open to test.) Cool. Taste and add more salt if desired.

Spinach Ball Appetizers
Makes several dozen

2	10 oz. pkg. frozen spinach, chopped, cooked, drained, and squeezed dry
2	cups stuffing mix, ground fine
2	medium onions, chopped fine
1	8 oz. can water chestnuts, drained and chopped
2	eggs, beaten
¾	cup melted butter
½	cup grated Parmesan cheese
1	tbsp. garlic powder
½	tsp. thyme (optional)
½	tsp. pepper

Preheat oven to 350°.

1. Combine all ingredients in large bowl, and mix well.

2. Shape into bite-sized balls, and place onto ungreased cookie sheet.

3. Bake for 20 minutes.

These are good either hot out of oven or served cold.

Sugar and Nut Glazed Brie
Serves six to eight

¼   cup packed brown sugar
¼   cup coarsely chopped mixed nuts (walnuts, pecans, almonds, filberts, etc.)
1   tbsp. brandy
1   14 oz. round Brie cheese, about 5" in diameter, chilled apple wedges, grapes, pear slices, crackers

1. Stir together sugar, nuts and brandy in a small bowl. Microwave uncovered on high about one minute or until sugar is melted.

2. Place chilled cheese on platter or glass pie plate. Spread sugar-and-nut mixture over cheese. Microwave, uncovered, on 50 percent power about 1½ minutes or until cheese is heated through but not melted.

Arrange fruit and crackers around cheese to serve.

Make sure cheese is well chilled so it softens inside, but does not melt. Microwave settings may need to be adjusted depending on wattage of the oven.

Sweet Nibbles

2	tbsp. oil
1	lb. white chocolate
3	cups mini pretzels
2	cups raisins
2	cups dry roasted peanuts

1. Melt white chocolate with oil in large saucepan.

2. Stir in pretzels, raisins and peanuts (other nuts and dried fruits may be used).

3. Line a 9" x 13" baking dish with foil and pour in hot mixture.

4. Place in refrigerator until cold.

5. Remove and break into small pieces. Store in cool place.

A simple, fun and tasty treat. Place in decorative jars or tins and give as gifts.

Schweitzer
Foster Cline, MD.

Breads & Breakfasts

Schweitzer Ski Area, circa 1964
Jim Parsons Jr. Collection

Schweitzer Ski Area, circa 1964
Jim Parsons Jr. Collection

Apple Upside Down French Toast

Serves eight

5	tbsp. butter
2	large baking apples, peeled, cored and sliced
1	cup firmly packed dark brown sugar
2	tbsp. dark corn syrup
1	tsp. cinnamon
1	large loaf French bread, cut into eight 1" slices
3	large eggs or egg substitutes
1	cup milk
1	tsp. vanilla

1. The day before, melt butter in large skillet over medium heat. Add apple slices and cook, stirring occasionally until tender. Add brown sugar, corn syrup and cinnamon. Cook and stir until sugar dissolves. Pour into 9" x 13" baking dish and spread evenly.

2. Arrange bread slices in one layer over top of apples. In separate bowl, beat eggs, milk and vanilla. Pour over bread. Cover and refrigerate over night.

3. The next day, heat oven to 375°. Remove cover and bake 30 to 35 minutes or until mixture is firm and bread is golden. Cool in pan 5 minutes and invert on serving plate so that the apples and syrup are on top.

4. More egg milk mixture may be needed so that bread is well saturated to keep finished dish from being too dry. Also you can reduce amount of brown sugar to ¾ cup. Sprinkle with chopped pecans & cinnamon.

Apricot Nut Bread
Single loaf

1	cup dried apricots, chopped
1	cup sugar
2	tbsp. shortening
1	egg, beaten
¼	cup granulated sugar
½	cup orange juice
2	cups sifted flour
2	tsp. baking powder
½	tsp. salt
1	cup walnuts, chopped

Preheat oven to 350°.

1. Soak dried apricots for 20 minutes in water. Cream together ¾ cup sugar, shortening and egg. Stir in remaining ¼ cup sugar and orange juice. Add dry ingredients (except nuts), and stir until smooth.

2. Drain apricots, and add to mixture along with nuts. Pour batter into greased and floured loaf pan, and bake for 65 minutes or until done. Use a skewer to test for doneness.

3. Slice thin and serve plain, or spread with butter or cream cheese. Also good toasted. Store in refrigerator or freeze.

1937 Snow
Jim Parsons Jr. Collection

Basque Sheepherders Bread
Single loaf

3	cups hot water
½	cup butter or margarine
½	cup sugar
2½	tsp. salt
2	tbsp. yeast
9½	cups flour
	salad oil

1. Combine water, butter, sugar and salt in saucepan, and heat until butter melts. Add yeast and 5 cups of flour and beat until smooth. Add remaining flour and knead or beat again until smooth. Let rise one and a half hours in very large bowl. (To speed this up, pre-warm bowl in oven; turn off and let dough rise in bowl.)

2. After dough has risen, punch down and knead to form a smooth ball. Cut circle of foil to cover bottom of heavy 4 quart Dutch oven with lid. Cut two small strips of foil to cover the handles of Dutch oven. Grease (slather) Dutch oven rim and lid with salad oil, and apply foil.

3. Grease top of foil in pan bottom. Place in warm oven just long enough to warm Dutch oven and lid. Remove and add dough. Let rise until dough just begins to lift lid.(It really will!) This takes about an hour. If dough rises too much it will tilt as bread continues to rise. Watch closely.

4. With lid on, bake bread at 375° for 12 minutes. Remove lid and bake for 30 to 35 minutes. It is done when it sounds hollow when tapped.

5. Invert Dutch oven and bread should just fall out (if pan has been adequately greased). If not, set pan upright, and slip dinner knife around edges and handles to loosen. Serve.

A showstopper! But tradition requires that you slash top with a cross and give first piece to dog.

Bean Bread
3 loaves

2	pkg. dry yeast
½	cup warm water
1	cup cooked navy or pea beans
½	cup nonfat dry milK
5	tbsp. sugar
7	cups flour
1	tbsp. salt
6	tsp. butter, melted

1. Dissolve yeast in warm water with a little sugar. In a blender, pureé beans with 1 cup of water. In a large bowl, mix pureé, 2 cups water, dry milk, sugar and salt. Stir in dissolved yeast and 2 cups flour. Beat until smooth. Mix in enough of remaining flour to make dough easy to handle.

2. Turn dough out on a lightly floured board and knead until smooth and elastic. (Add flour as needed to keep from being sticky.) Place dough in a greased bowl. Cover and let rise until double. Punch down the dough and divide into thirds. Shape each into an oval loaf and place on greased baking sheet. Let loaves rise until double.

3. Put loaves in 350° oven for one hour. Cool on rack. Brush top with butter for softer crust.

Caramel & Walnut Oven Baked French Toast
Serves eight

1½	cups packed brown sugar
¾	cup butter or margarine
4	tbsp. light corn syrup
1	cup walnuts, chopped
36-40	thick slices of baguette style French bread or
18	½" thick pieces of Sourdough or French bread (You may need less bread.)
6	eggs, beaten
1½	cups milk
1	tsp. vanilla

1. In saucepan combine brown sugar, butter and corn syrup to prepare the caramel sauce. Heat and stir until butter melts and brown sugar dissolves. Pour into a 10" x 14" pan. Add ½ cup walnuts.

2. Arrange enough bread slices to cover this mixture. Sprinkle with the rest of walnuts and top with another layer of bread slices.

3. Beat together eggs, milk and vanilla. Pour over bread. Press down lightly with spoon.

4. Cover with foil and chill overnight.

5. Bake uncovered at 350° for 30 to 40 minutes.

Let stand 10 minutes. Invert and place on serving platter.

A great prepare ahead "Company" recipe.

51

Cheddar Cheese Soufflé

Serves six

1	tbsp. softened butter
6	eggs
½	cup heavy cream
¼	cup Parmesan cheese, grated
½	tsp. prepared mustard
½	tsp. salt
¼	tsp. pepper
½	lb. sharp Cheddar cheese
11	oz. cream cheese

Preheat oven 375°.

1. Butter 5 cup soufflé dish or another deep baking dish. Place eggs, cream, Parmesan, mustard, salt and pepper in blender. Whirl until smooth.

2. Cut Cheddar cheese into pieces and add piece by piece to blender. Cut cream cheese into pieces and add to container. When all cheeses have been added, whirl mixture at high speed for 5 seconds.

3. Pour soufflé mixture into prepared dish and bake for 45 minutes for a soft, liquid center or 50 minutes for a firm soufflé. (The soft, liquid center is particularly delicious because it serves as a built-in sauce to spoon over soufflé.)

4. If you use individual soufflé dishes, bake for 15 to 20 minutes. The top will be golden brown and slightly cracked when baked to the maximum time.

This can be made ahead of time and refrigerated.

Photographer, Dr. Page, circa 1940's
Jim Parsons Jr. Collection

Cheddar Garlic Portabella Soufflé

Serves four

4	large portabella mushrooms
2½	tbsp. butter
3	tbsp. fine dry bread crumbs
1½	tbsp. garlic, minced
¼	cup all-purpose flour
¼	tsp. salt
¼	tsp. pepper
¾	cup milk
1¼	cups sharp Cheddar cheese, shredded
4	large eggs, separated

Preheat oven to 375°.

1. Wipe mushrooms. Remove stems and finely chop. Set caps, smooth side down, on a 12" x 15" baking sheet.

2. Cut 4 sheets of foil, each 12" x 16". Fold each sheet in half lengthwise, then again to make a 3 x 16 inch strip. Butter one side of each strip and dust with bread crumbs.

3. Tightly wrap each foil strip, crumb side in, around a mushroom cap, overlapping ends; secure with paper clips.

4. Sauté garlic and chopped mushroom stems in 2 tbsp. butter until stems are browned and limp. Add flour, salt and pepper and stir 1 minute. Remove from heat and add milk, whisking until smooth. Stir over high heat until boiling. Remove from heat. Add

54

1 cup cheese and stir until melted. Add egg yolks and stir to blend.

5. Whip egg whites until stiff, but not dry. Stir about ⅓ of whites into cheese mixture to lighten; then gently fold cheese mixture into remaining whites just until blended. Spoon mixture onto mushroom caps and sprinkle with remaining cheese.

6. Bake until soufflés are well browned, about 30 minutes. Cut foil strips and gently peel away. Transfer soufflés to plates with a spatula and serve immediately.

Good for brunch, lunch or light supper with salad.

Chili Corn Bread

Serves nine

2	large eggs
¼	cup corn oil
1	cup stone ground yellow cornmeal
2	tsp. baking powder
½	cup sour cream
8	oz. can creamed style corn
4	oz. can chopped green chilies, drained
6	oz. sharp Cheddar cheese, grated medium fine

Preheat oven to 350°.

1. Beat eggs until foamy; add oil, cornmeal, baking powder and sour cream; beat until smooth.

2. Stir in corn, chilies and cheese. Turn into a buttered 8" x 8" x 2" baking dish. Bake until cake tester inserted in center comes out clean, about one hour. Serve warm.

Church Street House Fall French Toast

Serves four to six

½	cup milk
¾	cup half and half
3	eggs
1	tsp. orange zest, grated
2	tbsp. brown sugar
½	tsp. ginger, freshly grated
½	tsp. cinnamon
¼	tsp. nutmeg
1	tsp. vanilla
1	cup pumpkin, mashed
6	slices egg bread or sweet French bread, 1" thick
½	cup pecan halves, roasted for 15 minutes in 325 ° oven
½	tbsp. unsalted butter (for top)
1	tsp. unsalted butter, room temperature for buttering dish

1. Butter a 9" x 13" baking dish and set aside. Mix first 10 ingredients (up to and including pumpkin). Pour small amount in bottom of dish, just enough to cover. Arrange sliced bread in dish, and pour custard over bread, cover with foil, and refrigerate 8 to 24 hours.

2. Just before baking at 350°, dot with butter, and bake covered. When bread becomes puffy, remove foil (after about an hour). Bake for another 15 minutes.

3. Cut on diagonal, top with roasted pecans and maple syrup. Unique and delicious.

Crème Brûlée French Toast

Serves six

½   cup unsalted butter
1   cup brown sugar, packed
2   tbsp. corn syrup
1   8-9" round loaf French bread
5   large eggs
1½   cups half and half
1   tsp. vanilla
1   tsp. Grand Marnier
¼   tsp. salt

1. Melt butter with brown sugar and corn syrup over medium heat in a small, heavy saucepan, stirring until smooth. Pour into 13" x 9" x 2" baking dish. Cut six 1" thick slices from center portion of bread, reserving ends for another use, and trim crusts. Arrange bread slices in one layer in baking dish, squeezing slightly to fit.

2. In another bowl, whisk together eggs, half and half, vanilla, Grand Marnier, and salt until well combined, and pour evenly over bread. Cover bread mixture, and chill for at least 8 hours and up to 1 day.

3. Bring bread mixture to room temperature. Bake uncovered in middle of oven at 350° until puffed and edges are pale golden, 35 to 40 minutes.

4. Serve immediately.

Eggnog Scones

Makes 16 scones

3	cups all-purpose flour
¼	cup sugar
2	tsp. baking powder
1	tsp. baking soda
½	tsp salt
¼	tsp. ground nutmeg
½	cup butter, cut in pieces
1¼	cups prepared eggnog
¾	cup dried cranberries
1	tsp. orange rind, grated
2	tbsp. milk
	sprinkle with sugar

Preheat oven to 425°.

1. Prepare Dough: Combine first 6 ingredients in food processor; mix well. Cut butter into flour mixture. Pour mixture into bowl. Make a well in center of dry mixture; add eggnog. Stir with fork until just combined. Add cranberries and orange rind.

2. Gather dough and divide into two balls to make scones. Roll or pat one ball on floured surface to form a circle ¾ inch thick. Cut into 8 pie-shaped pieces. Place on lightly greased baking sheet. Repeat with remaining dough. Brush with milk and sprinkle with sugar.

3. Bake 12 minutes or until tops are browned.

Eggs Mornay
Serves eight

1   dozen hard-boiled eggs

Sauce

4   tbsp. butter
½   cup flour
1   tsp. salt
¼   tsp. pepper
      pinch cayenne
3   cups hot milk
4   tbsp. grated Parmesan cheese
½   cup grated Swiss cheese

Filling

4   tbsp. butter
½   lb. mushrooms, finely chopped
2   tbsp. parsley, chopped
½   tsp. dry tarragon

Topping

1   cup bread crumbs
2   tbsp. melted butter
2   tbsp. Parmesan cheese

Preheat oven to 350°.

1. Peel eggs and cut in half. Remove yolks and place whites aside. Mash yolks and reserve.

2. For cheese sauce melt butter and whisk in flour a little at a time. Stir constantly to prevent lumps; cook until thickened. Add salt, pepper, cayenne, Parmesan and Swiss cheeses; stir until melted. Remove from heat and set aside.

3. For filling, sauté mushrooms and butter until mixture is almost dry. Add chopped parsley and tarragon, and add mixture to the mashed egg yolks. Stir in ½ cup of cheese sauce.

4. Fill egg whites with mixture. Spread small layer of cheese sauce in shallow baking dish. Place egg halves in a baking dish, and spoon remaining sauce over top. Finish with thick layer of bread crumbs.

5. Bake for 30 minutes, or cover and refrigerate and bake later. Heating time will take longer if dish is cold when put in oven.

Fruit and Nut Muffins
18 large muffins

1	cup applesauce
1	cup sugar
¼	cup olive oil
2	eggs
3	tbsp. skim or buttermilk
1	cup unbleached flour
½	cup soy flour
½	cup wheat germ or wheat bran
1	tsp. baking powder
1	tsp. baking soda
1	tsp. cinnamon
½	cup walnuts, chopped
1	medium apple peeled, cored and chopped
1	cup fresh cranberries

Topping

¼	cup unbleached flour
¼	cup sugar
¼	tsp. cinnamon
¼	tsp. butter

Preheat oven to 350°.

1. In a large bowl combine applesauce, sugar, oil, milk and eggs. Add flour, baking soda, baking powder and cinnamon. Mix well. Stir in nuts, apples and cranberries until mixed.

2. For streusel topping mix flour, sugar and cinnamon. Cut in butter until mixture is crumbly.

3. Spoon muffin mix into lined muffin tins until ¾ full. Sprinkle with the streusel topping. Additional chopped nuts also may be sprinkled on top. Bake at 350° for about 20 minutes. Cool on a rack.

Substitute raisins or dates for cranberries.

Fiesta Soufflé
Serves sixteen

24	eggs
1½	containers (24 oz.) cottage cheese
1½	bags (16 oz.) Monterey Jack cheese
1	cup flour
2¼	tsp. baking powder
¼	cup butter, melted
6	green onions, sliced
1	small can chopped green chilies (optional)
1	small can sliced black olives
3	small jar pimientos, chopped

Garnish with Cheddar cheese, sour cream or salsa

Preheat oven to 350°.

1. Mix ingredients in large bowl. Pour mixture into greased 10" x 15" pan or 16 ramekins. (May be refrigerated overnight at this point.) Bake for 35 to 40 minutes. (Allow soufflé batter to stand at room temperature for 20 minutes before baking.)

2. Serve.

Expecting a crowd for breakfast or brunch? Try this.

Garden Angel Biscuits
Makes twelve to fourteen biscuits

1	pkg. dry yeast
2	tbsp. warm water
2½	cups flour
1	tbsp. sugar
1½	tsp. baking powder
½	tsp. baking soda
¼	tsp. salt
½	cup shortening
¼	cup carrot, finely shredded
1	tbsp. snipped parsley
2	tbsp. green onion, finely chopped
1	cup buttermilk

Preheat oven to 450°.

1. Mix yeast and water in bowl. In large bowl, mix together dry ingredients, then cut in shortening. Stir carrots, parsley and green onions into flour mixture. Add buttermilk and yeast mixture. Using fork, stir until moistened. Turn dough out onto floured surface. Quickly knead for 6 to 8 strokes, or until nearly smooth. Pat or roll into ½" thickness. Cut with floured biscuit cutter.

2. Place on ungreased baking sheet and bake for 10 to 12 minutes.

German Apple Oven Pancakes
Serves four

¼   cup butter or margarine
4   eggs
¾   cup flour
¾   cup milk
½   tsp. salt
2   medium apples, peeled and sliced
¼   cup sugar
¼   tsp. cinnamon

Preheat oven to 400°.

1. Melt butter in a 9" pan. Mix together eggs, flour, milk, salt. When butter is melted pour in egg mixture. Slice apples on top of egg mixture. Sprinkle top with cinnamon and sugar.

2. Bake about 35 to 40 minutes or until egg mixture is set and crust is golden brown.

This is a special breakfast or evening meal. Kids love these pancakes. If you want a plain German Oven Pancake just omit apples and bake.

Herb Butter Spread Bread

Serves eight to ten

1	loaf unsliced French bread
½	tsp. Worcestershire
¾	cup butter, softened
½	tsp. salt
½	tsp. whole leaf dried thyme
½	tsp. whole leaf dried marjoram

Preheat oven to 325°.

1. Cut off top, side and end crusts of bread. Leaving the bottom crust attached, cut bread in half lengthwise and into ¾" pieces crosswise. Cream butter, salt and Worcestershire. Crush thyme and marjoram leaves, add to butter and mix well. Spread all cut surfaces of bread, inside and out, with butter.

2. Place bread on rimmed baking sheet (butter will run as it heats). Bake uncovered for 30 minutes or until crisp. Serve hot.

A new way of serving bread at a dinner party.

Individual Applesauce Soufflé
Serves four

1½	cups unsweetened applesauce
1	tbsp honey
½	tsp. cinnamon
1	tbsp. raisins
3	egg whites

Preheat oven to 350°.

1. Blend 4 tablespoons applesauce with honey and cinnamon. Spoon 1 tablespoon applesauce into bottom of each of four greased, six ounce custard cups or ramekins. Top with raisins.

2. Beat egg whites until stiff, but not dry. Fold half into remaining applesauce, and blend well. Gently fold remaining whites into this mixture. Spoon into custard cups. Sprinkle top with cinnamon.

3. Bake in upper third of oven for about 20 minutes, until puffed and lightly browned.

Serve immediately.

Lemon Blueberry Bread
Makes one loaf

1½	cups flour
1	tsp. baking powder
½	tsp.salt
⅓	cup butter
1	cup sugar
3	tbsp. lemon juice
2	eggs
½	cup milk
2	tbsp. grated lemon peel
½	cup nuts, chopped
1	cup blueberries, fresh or frozen

Glaze

2	tbsp. lemon juice
¼	cup sugar

Preheat oven to 350°.

1. Combine flour, baking powder and salt in small bowl and set aside. Cream butter, sugar, lemon juice and eggs; add flour mixture ½ at a time, alternating with milk. Fold in lemon peel, nuts and blueberries. Pour mixture into greased, floured bread pan.

2. Bake for 60 to 70 minutes, or until center of bread springs back when pressed. Cool in pan 10 minutes.

3. While bread is cooling, combine lemon juice with sugar. Remove bread from pan to wire rack. Drizzle with glaze.

Oatmeal Huckleberry Muffins
Serves twelve

2⅔	cups flour
1½	cups quick oatmeal
4	tsp. baking powder
1	tsp. baking soda
½	tsp. salt
2	eggs
1½	cups milk
1	cup brown sugar
½	cup oil
1	tsp. vanilla
1	cup huckleberries
1	cup pecans, chopped

Preheat oven to 400°.

1. Mix together first five ingredients in a bowl. Make a well in the center. Add eggs, milk, brown sugar, oil and vanilla to dry mixture. Stir until moistened (it will be lumpy). Fold in berries and nuts.

2. Spoon into prepared muffin cups, filling each ¾ full. Bake for 16 to 18 minutes. Cool in muffin cups for five minutes then remove.

Frozen berries can be used in this recipe. It also makes great mini muffins (bake 10 to 12 minutes). Consider adding grated orange peel for more flavor.

Black Tail Mountain, looking up at the Clark Fork, 1950
Jim Parsons Jr. Collection

Pistachio Scones

Makes 12 large scones

2¼	cups flour
2	cups cornmeal
¾	cup sugar
¾	cup chopped, unsalted roasted pistachios or walnuts, chopped
1	tbsp. baking powder
½	tsp. salt
¼	pound butter
1⅓	cups milk plus 2 more tbsp.
1	tbsp. grated lemon peel or 2 tsp. lemon extract
1	large egg yolk
	sugar to sprinkle on the top of scones

Preheat to 375°.

1. In a large bowl mix flour, corn meal, sugar, nuts, baking powder and salt.

2. Cut butter into chunks and add to mixture in bowl. With your fingers or pastry blender cut butter into mixture until it forms coarse crumbs.

3. Add 1⅓ cups milk and lemon to mixture and stir with a fork until evenly moistened.

4. Turn dough out onto floured board and knead until dough holds together. (It will be sticky.)

5. Divide the dough in half and form into a ball. Pat each ball into a 7" round that is about 1" thick. Cut

each round into about 6 sections.

6. Place wedges 2" apart on buttered 14" x 17" baking sheet. Beat egg yolk with remaining 2 tablespoons of milk just to blend. Brush tops of wedges with egg mixture and sprinkle lightly with sugar.
7. Bake in middle rack until scones are lightly browned or about 25 minutes.

8. Serve warm with orange marmalade, honey or butter.

Rhubarb Strawberry Coffee Cake

Serves ten to twelve

Filling

3	cups frozen, unsweetened rhubarb (thawed) cut into 1" pieces
16	oz. frozen, or 2 cups fresh, sliced strawberries
2	tbsp. lemon juice
⅓	cup cornstarch

Cake Batter

3	cups flour
1	cup sugar
1	tsp. baking soda
1	tsp. baking powder
1	tsp. salt
1	cup butter
1	cup buttermilk
2	eggs, beaten
1	tsp. vanilla

Topping

¾	cup sugar
½	cup flour
½	cup butter

Preheat oven to 350°.

Make filling first and cool.

1. Make filling in a saucepan. Combine rhubarb and strawberries. Cook for 4 minutes. Then add lemon juice. Combine the sugar with cornstarch, add to rhubarb mixture. Stir while cooking about 5 minutes

until mixture is thick and bubbly. Let cool while preparing the cake.

2. In large bowl, mix together flour, sugar, baking soda, baking powder and salt. Cut in 1 cup of butter. Beat buttermilk, eggs and vanilla together, and add to dry mixture, stirring just until moistened. Do not over mix. Pour ½ of the batter into a buttered 10" x 14" pan, spreading evenly. Spread cooled filling on top of batter. Spoon remaining batter, in small mounds, onto filling.

3. For the topping mix sugar and flour together and cut in remaining butter. Sprinkle topping over batter and bake for 45 minutes.

Sandpoint Interurban Railway, photo 1912. It ran from November 15, 1909 to mid November, 1917. Route was from Lincoln School to Ponderay.

Snickerdoodle Mini Muffins
Makes three dozen

1½   cups flour
1   cup Quaker Oats (quick or old-fashioned)
½   cup sugar
1   tbsp. baking powder
1   cup fat-free milk
1   egg, lightly beaten
4   tbsp. margarine or butter, melted
1   tsp. vanilla

For muffin topping

⅓   cup sugar
1   tsp. cinnamon
       mix well in a bowl

Preheat oven to 400°.

1. Combine flour, oats, sugar and baking powder in large bowl; mix well.

2. In small bowl, combine milk, egg, margarine and vanilla. Blend well. Add this mixture to dry ingredients. Stir until mixed. (Do not over stir.)

3. Fill muffin cups ¾ full. Sprinkle topping evenly over muffins.

4. Bake 12 to 14 minutes. Cool muffins on wire rack for 5 minutes. Serve warm.

Soft Pretzels
Makes 18 pretzels

1	pkg. dry yeast
1½	cups warm water
1	tsp. salt
1	tbsp. sugar
4	cups flour
1	egg, beaten
	coarse salt

Preheat oven to 425°.

1. Dissolve yeast in 1½ cups warm water. Stir in salt and sugar.

2. Blend in 4 cups flour. Knead dough until smooth. Cut into 18 small pieces. Roll into ropes and twist into desired shapes. Place on lightly greased cookie sheet. Brush each pretzel with beaten egg and sprinkle with coarse salt.

3. Bake for 12 to 15 minutes.

4. For hard pretzels reduce water to 1¼ cup. Add ¼ cup melted butter and make pretzels smaller in size. Bake until brown.

These will keep for several days.

Walnut Bread
Makes one loaf

2	cups flour
⅓	cup sugar
1	tbsp. baking powder
½	tsp. salt
1	egg
1	cup milk
⅓	cup canola oil
2	cups toasted walnuts, chopped

Preheat oven to 350°.

1. Stir together flour, sugar, baking powder and salt. Make a well in the center of flour mixture; set aside.

2. In a medium bowl beat egg, stir in milk and oil.

3. Add egg mixture all at once to flour mixture.

4. Stir until mixture is moist. (Batter should be lumpy.) Fold in the nuts. Spoon batter into greased 8" x 4" x 2" loaf pan.

5. Bake for 50 to 55 minutes or until wooden toothpick inserted comes out clean.

6. Cool in pan on a wire rack for 10 minutes. Remove from pan and cool completely.

Walnut bread is an excellent accompaniment with Cheddar cheese and glass of wine.

Walter Burt 1949
Walter Burt Collection

Sourdough Point
Brendan Rodgers

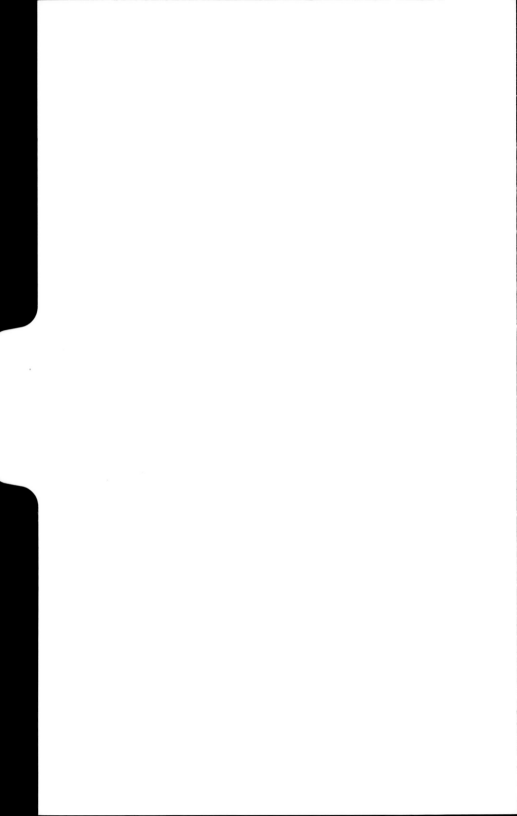

Soups

Page Hospital, circa 1920
Jim Parsons Jr. Collection

March 12, 1911
Bonner Country Historical Society Collection

Black Bean Soup
Serves six to eight

16	oz. dried black beans
6	cups chicken broth
2	tbsp. butter, unsalted
1	cup onion, chopped
1	cup carrots, shredded
1	cup celery, chopped
1	cup potato, diced
1	bay leaf
1	tsp. salt
½	tsp. garlic powder
1	tsp. oregano
¼	tsp. pepper
3	tbsp.lemon juice

1. Soak beans as directed on package. Drain. Add beans to chicken broth and boil 1½ hours. Melt butter and sauté onion, carrots, celery and potatoes. Add sautéed ingredients and seasonings to beans.

2. Simmer for one hour.

3. Stir in lemon juice and serve.

Cabbage Sausage Soup
Serves six to eight

1	14.5 oz. can tomatoes, diced
1	lb. Kielbasa sausage, cut up
½	medium cabbage, shredded
4	medium carrots, sliced
3	medium potatoes, cubed
3	celery stalks, sliced
1	turnip, cubed
1	large onion, sliced
2	quarts beef stock (or 2 quarts water and 1 package onion soup mix and 3 beef bouillon cubes.)
1	6 oz. can tomato paste
2	tbsp. vinegar
1	tsp. salt
½	tsp. thyme

1. Cook all ingredients in a soup pot for 1 hour.

Cabbage Sausage Soup is hearty, cold-weather soup. It is almost a stew. Pair with a crusty bread and a fresh green salad.

Carrot Soup
Serves four

3	tbsp. butter
1	lb. carrots, peeled and diced
1	small onion, chopped
1	medium potato, peeled and diced
½	tsp. salt
¼	tsp. freshly ground black pepper
½	tsp. sugar
3	cups beef broth

Garnish

1	tsp. chervil or marjoram, chopped
1	tbsp. parsley, chopped

1. Melt butter in heavy saucepan. Add carrots, onion and potato. Season with salt, pepper and sugar. Cover and cook over low heat for 15 minutes.

2. Add broth and bring to a boil. Lower heat, cover and simmer for another 15 minutes.

3. Put soup in a blender or force through a sieve.

4. Serve hot or cold. Garnish each bowl with chopped herbs.

Cauliflower Cheese Soup
Serves six

1	medium cauliflower, coarsely chopped
¼	cup butter
⅔	cup onion, chopped
1	large garlic clove, minced
1	cup flour
2	cups chicken broth, cold
1	cup liquid reserved from drained cauliflower
1	cup light cream
½	tsp. Worcestershire sauce
2	shakes Tabasco
½	tsp. or more prepared horseradish
¾	tsp. salt
	ground pepper to taste
1	cup sharp Cheddar cheese, grated
	chives or parsley, chopped
	paprika to garnish

1. Cook cauliflower until crispy tender in boiling salted water; drain, reserving liquid. Melt butter in 3 quart sauce pan. Add onion and garlic, cook until soft. Blend in flour. Stir in cold chicken broth and 1 cup reserved liquid. Bring to a boil; add light cream until soup is desired consistency.

2. Add Worcestershire sauce, Tabasco, horseradish, salt and pepper. Add cauliflower to soup and simmer 5 minutes. Remove from heat and add grated cheese. Serve with a sprinkle of paprika and chopped chives or parsley.

Helen "Pete" Peterson was born in Sandpoint March 31, 1913. She was known to all as *Dr. Pete*. She graduated from Sandpoint High in 1930. It took 7 years to earn her BS. She received her MA in Bacteriology and Public Health from Washington State College. In 1939 she enrolled in Case Western Reserve University in Cleveland, Ohio, to study medicine. On occasion she had to sell her blood to make ends meet. She interned at University Hospital and did her residency at Lutheran Hospital in Cleveland. While there she was the first woman to be named Chief Surgical Resident. In 1943, she finished her medical training and returned to Sandpoint to practice medicine.

Chestnut Soup
Serves Six

1	lb. chestnuts
1	shallot, diced
1	celery root, peeled and diced
1	stalk celery, diced
½	lb. unsalted butter
2	cups heavy cream
2	cups chicken stock

Preheat oven to 400°.

1. Score chestnuts and roast them for about 20 minutes.

2. Peel chestnuts and reserve six for garnish. Dice the rest.

3. In sauté pan over medium heat melt butter. Add shallot, celery root and stock. Sauté for about 10 minutes or until golden.

4. Add chestnuts and sauté for 5 more minutes.

5. Add cream and chicken stock. Let simmer for 20 minutes.

6. Pureé soup in blender.

7. Serve in hot soup bowls. Garnish with remaining whole chestnuts.

This is Thanksgiving tradition at our house.

Chicken Soup with Brown Rice

Serves six

5	cups chicken broth
3	carrots, peeled and cut into ¼" pieces
1	celery stalk, peeled and cut into ¼" pieces
1	sweet potato, peeled and cut into ¼" pieces
1	tsp. salt
2	cups cooked chicken, cut into bite-size pieces
1	cup brown rice, cooked

1. In a 3 quart saucepan, combine chicken broth, carrots, celery, sweet potato and salt. Bring to a boil, then reduce heat and simmer until the vegetables are tender, about 15 minutes. Add chicken and rice. Heat through and serve.

Chicken Soup with Brown Rice is quick, easy and nutritious.

Olive Mayo Nelson, circa 1950s
James Parsons Collection

Chicken, Sausage & Shrimp Gumbo

Serves eight to twelve

1	3 lb. roasting chicken, cut up
	salt, garlic powder, and cayenne
	oil for frying
3	cups chicken stock
4	cups water
½	tsp. thyme
½	tsp. oregano
2	bay leaves
½	cup flour
1½	medium onions, chopped
1	green pepper, chopped
1½	celery stalks, chopped
2	cloves garlic, minced
1	14 oz. can plum tomatoes in purée
1-2	tsp. cayenne, depending on taste
1	tsp. Worcestershire sauce
2	tbsp. gumbo file'
½	bag sliced okra
¾	lb. Andouille smoked sausage, sliced
½	lb. medium shrimp, shelled

1. Remove excess fat from chicken. Rub generous amount of salt, garlic powder and cayenne on each piece. Brown chicken in oil, transfer it to large pot as it is browned.

2. Add broth, water, herbs and bay leaves. Bring broth to a boil and lower to simmer for one hour or until chicken is tender.

3. Remove chicken. When cool bone and cut meat into bite-sized pieces.

4. While chicken is cooking, pour off fat from frying pan, measure and return ½ cup fat and browned particles to pan.

5. Place pan over medium heat and add ½ cup of flour, stirring constantly. Cook over medium heat until roux is a nice brown color. Add chopped vegetable mixture, onions, peppers, celery and garlic. Cook about five minutes.

6. Add this mixture to hot broth, spoonful by spoonful, stirring constantly. Add tomatoes, cayenne, Worcestershire and gumbo file'. Cook 20 to 30 minutes.

7. Meanwhile, sauté okra and sausage in oil and add to gumbo pot. Cook about an hour. Just before serving, add chicken and shrimp. Taste for seasoning.

8. Pour gumbo over rice and serve.

This recipe is gumbo-lover's delight.

Optional: Add 1 cup of fish stock to broth, or tie shrimp shells in cheesecloth and cook in broth. Remove before serving.

Cinco De Mayo Soup
Serves eight to ten

5   pork chops (boneless)
2   cups all-purpose flour
2   tbsp. oil
4   14-oz. cans chicken broth
1   medium onion, peeled and diced
4   cloves garlic (or more)
2   tsp. dry oregano
3-4   15 oz. cans yellow (or white) hominy, drained
1   small can chopped green chilies
2   cups water
      salt and pepper to taste

Condiments
grated cheese
chopped green onions
sour cream
cilantro
avocado
shredded lettuce
shredded radishes
crushed tortilla chips
chopped tomatoes

1. Trim fat from pork chops and cut into small pieces. Place meat into bag with flour and shake. Heat oil in a large kettle; add meat and brown. Add remaining ingredients and simmer one hour.

2. Serve with a selection of condiments.

Crab Bisque
Serves four

12	oz. crab meat
2	tbsp. onion, grated
2	tbsp. butter
2	tbsp. flour
¼	tsp. celery salt
2	tsp. parsley, minced
1	cup chicken broth
2	cups milk

1. In a large saucepan, sauté onions in butter. Stir in flour, celery salt and parsley. Cook until smooth and bubbly. Remove from heat and gradually stir in chicken broth and milk. Bring to a boil for about 1 minute, reduce heat and stir in crab meat. Salt and pepper to taste. Heat to a serving temperature.

2. Garnish with fresh parsley and serve.

This is an easy and excellent soup.

Creamy Seafood Bisque
Serves 6

6	tbsp. butter
1	medium onion, chopped
1	cup celery with leaves, chopped
5	tbsp. flour
3	cups chicken stock
2	cups light cream or 2% milk
½	cup dry white wine or vermouth
1	tbsp. parsley, chopped
	dash or two of Tabasco
1	tsp. paprika
1	tsp. salt or to taste
¼	tsp. white pepper
1	lb. cooked seafood (crab, scallops, shrimp, salmon, halibut)

1. In large pot, melt butter. Sauté onion and celery until tender. Blend in flour and gradually whisk in chicken stock, cream and wine. Stir constantly until soup thickens. DO NOT BOIL.

2. Season with parsley, Tabasco sauce and paprika. Salt and pepper to taste. Gently fold in seafood and heat throughly over low heat.

3. Serve immediately.

A good way to use leftover fish. Also can add cubed baked potato.

Elegant Mushroom Soup
Serves four

1	lb. mushrooms, trimmed and coarsely chopped
4	green onions with tops, coarsely chopped
8	tbsp. butter
⅓	cup flour
¼	tsp. dry mustard
1½	tsp. salt or to taste
	dash cayenne to taste
¼	tsp. freshly ground black pepper
2	cups chicken broth
2	cups half and half
⅓	cup sherry, optional

1. Sauté mushrooms, onion and green onions in butter in a large sauce pan for about 5 minutes.

2. Stir in flour, dry mustard, salt, cayenne, and black pepper.

3. Gradually stir in chicken broth and cream. (Can use 1 cup half and half and 1 cup milk.)

4. Simmer until thickened and smooth; stir constantly.

5. Add sherry if desired. Serve hot.

This is an elegant first course.

Elegant Winter Soup
Serves four to six

1½	cups onions, diced
3	tbsp. olive oil
1	tsp. garlic, minced
6	cups chicken broth
1	cup carrots, peeled and diced
1	cup sweet potatoes, peeled and diced
1	cup rutabaga, peeled and diced
1	cup celery root, peeled and diced
2	chicken breasts, cooked and diced
3	tbsp. tarragon
	salt and pepper

1. In a large saucepan, sauté onions in olive oil until soft. Add garlic, and cook on medium heat until golden. Add broth, carrots, sweet potatoes and rutabaga. Partially cover, and cook until vegetables are tender about 20 minutes. Add celery root and chicken, cook about 5 minutes more. Add tarragon, salt and pepper to taste. Cook another 5 minutes, until vegetables are soft but hold their shape.

2. Serve immediately.

Can be made up to 3 days ahead. Reheat slowly.

Fruit Soup

Serves ten to twelve

2	tbsp. tapioca
1½	cups water
2	tbsp. sugar
	dash salt
1	6-oz. can orange juice concentrate
1	pkg. each frozen strawberries and frozen raspberries, drained
1	can pineapple chunks, drained
1	large can peach slices, drained
1	can Mandarin oranges, drained
2	bananas

1. Combine tapioca and water and cook to a boil. Remove from heat; add sugar, salt and orange juice concentrate. Fold in drained fruits and chill. Just before serving fold in bananas.

2. Put in custard cups or for an elegant touch, champagne glasses and serve.

Good for brunch with French toast, Dutch Babies or similar breakfast entrée. Serve with Mimosas!

Greek Stew
Serves eight

3	lbs. beef chuck, trimmed and cut into 1½" cubes
	salt and pepper to taste
½	cup butter or oil
2½	lbs. small white onions, peeled and coarsely chopped
1	can six oz. tomato paste
⅔	cup red wine
2	tbsp. red wine vinegar
1	tbsp. light brown sugar
1	clove garlic, finely chopped
1	whole bay leaf
1	small cinnamon stick
½	tsp. whole cloves
½	tsp. ground cumin
2	tbsp. dried currants or raisins

1. In a large bowl, place the meat, seasoned with salt and pepper. In a heavy skillet over low heat melt butter or oil. Add meat and stir to coat with butter or oil, but do not let meat brown. Place onions over meat.

2. In a small bowl blend tomato paste, wine, red wine vinegar, brown sugar and garlic and pour over the beef and onion mixture.

3. Add bay leaf, cinnamon sick, whole cloves, cumin and currants or raisins.

4. Cover kettle with lid and simmer for 3 hours. Meat will be very tender.

5. Serve over buttered noodles.

Halibut Chowder
Serves 10 to 12

3	tbps. butter
2	cups onions, chopped
2	cloves garlic, minced
8	slices bacon (or ½ lb. of salt pork. Do not use smoky flavor.)
6	cups chicken stock
6	cups potatoes, peeled and diced
1	bay leaf
½	tsp. ground thyme
¼	tsp. allspice
2	tsp. salt
½	tsp. freshly ground black pepper
2	tbsp. fresh tarragon, chopped or 1 tbsp. dried
8	cups milk
3	tbsp. flour
½	cup clam juice
1½	lbs. halibut cut into 1" pieces

1. In a large frying pan melt butter and sauté onions, garlic and bacon or salt pork until onions are soft. Pour off fat and put mixture into large soup pot.

2. Add stock, potatoes, seasonings and milk. Bring to boil and simmer for 20 minutes or until potatoes are tender. Combine flour and clam juice and stir until smooth. Add to chowder stirring until chowder thickens and bubbles for one minute.

3. Add halibut chunks, cook for 3 minutes and serve.

Meaty Three Bean Chili
Serves ten to twelve

½	lb. hot Italian sausage
¼	lb. mild Italian sausage
¾	lb. ground beef
1	large onion, chopped
1	medium green pepper, chopped
1	jalapeño pepper, seeded and minced
2	garlic cloves, minced
1	cup beef broth
½	cup Worcestershire sauce
1½	tsp. chili powder
1	tsp. pepper
1	tsp. dry mustard
½	tsp. celery seed
½	tsp. salt
6	cups fresh plum tomatoes, chopped (or about 2 lbs.)
6	bacon strips, cooked and crumbled
1	can (15 oz.) kidney beans, rinsed and drained
1	can pinto beans, rinsed and drained
1	can (15 oz.) garbanzo beans rinsed and drained

1.   In a 4 quart kettle or Dutch oven, brown sausage and beef over medium heat. Drain and discard all but about 1 tablespoon of drippings. Set meat aside. Sauté onions, pepper, and garlic in drippings for about 3 minutes. Add beef broth, Worcestershire sauce and seasonings. Bring to a boil over medium heat.

2. Reduce heat, cover and simmer for 10 minutes. Add tomatoes, bacon, browned sausage and beef. Bring to a boil, reduce heat and simmer for 30 minutes. Add kidney, pinto, and garbanzo beans.

3. Simmer 1 hour, stirring occasionally.

4. Garnish with chopped onions if desired and serve.

My Brother's Easy Clam Chowder
Serves four to six

3	6½ oz. cans chopped or minced clams, drained
	water to cover vegetables
1	cup onion, finely chopped
1	cup celery, finely chopped
1	cup potatoes, finely chopped
¾	cup butter
¾	cup flour
1½	quarts whole milk
½	pint half and half
1½	tsp. salt
	pepper to taste

1. Pour clam juice over vegetables in large stock pot. Add enough water to barely cover vegetables. Simmer 45 minutes.

2. In a small sauce pan melt butter and add flour to make a roux. May brown butter before adding flour to enhance flavor. (Optional)

3. Slowly add milk and half and half making smooth gravy. Pour over vegetables. Add clams, salt and pepper to taste. Simmer 30 minutes.

Northwest Salmon Chowder

Serves four to six

½	cup each celery and onion, chopped
2	cloves garlic, minced
3	tbsp. olive oil
4	cups vegetable broth, canned or boxed
1	cup potatoes, diced, peeled or unpeeled
1	cup carrots, shredded
	salt and pepper to taste
1	tbsp. dill weed
1	15 oz. can creamed corn
1-2	cups half and half
1½-2	cups cooked salmon, approximately 1 lb.

Preheat oven to 350°.

1. Wrap salmon in foil and bake at 350° until it flakes.

2. In stock pot, sauté onion, celery and garlic in olive oil until tender. Add broth, potatoes, carrots, salt, pepper, and dill weed. Bring to boil. Reduce heat to low. Cover and simmer for 30 minutes or until vegetables are tender. Stir in corn, half and half and cooked salmon.

3. Simmer for 15 minutes or until heated through.

Oxtail Tomato Vegetable Soup

Serves six to eight

	flour for dredging
2	oxtails (about 3 lbs.) cut in pieces
2	tbsp. bacon drippings or oil
2¼	cups tomato juice or vegetable juice
3	cups water
1	tsp. lemon juice
½	cup each carrots, onions and celery, diced
1	cup potatoes, diced
1	tsp. salt
	dash pepper
1	tsp. Worcestershire sauce

1. Sprinkle meat with flour. Heat drippings or oil in a large pan. Add oxtails and slowly brown on all sides. Add tomato juice, water and lemon juice.

2. Cover and simmer gently for about 3 hours. Remove bones; add vegetables, salt, pepper and Worcestershire sauce. Cover and simmer for 30 to 45 minutes longer or until vegetables are as tender as you like. Season with more salt if necessary.

Barley makes a nice addition.

Potato, Bacon & Corn Chowder
Makes two quarts

¼	lb. bacon, chopped
	water as needed
1	large onion, chopped
1	cup celery, chopped
4	large potatoes, peeled and cubed
4	cups chicken stock
4	cups milk
¼	tsp. dill seed
1	cup corn (fresh or frozen)
6	tbsp. flour
1	cup water
	Salt and pepper to taste

1. In large soup pot cook bacon and drain off fat. Add onion and celery and sauté in a small amount of water until transparent. Add potatoes and chicken stock; simmer until potatoes are tender. Add milk, dill and corn.

2. Mix flour with water and whisk until smooth. Add to soup mixture a small amount at a time, until mixture thickens. Salt and pepper to taste and simmer 20 minutes.

Serve with Crostini and a glass of wine.

Pumpkin Soup
Serves eight to ten

¼	cup butter
1	onion, chopped
1	29 oz. can pumpkin
1	16 oz. can pumpkin
1	49 oz. can of chicken broth
1	12 oz. can evaporated milk
2	tsp. ground nutmeg
1	tsp. ground ginger
1	tbsp. ground curry
¼	tsp. salt
	a few dashes of hot pepper sauce

Garnish

sour cream
parsley

1. Melt butter and sauté onions.

2. Add pumpkin and gradually stir in chicken broth, evaporated milk and seasonings.

3. Bring to boil. Reduce heat and simmer uncovered for about 5 minutes.

4. Stir occasionally to blend flavors. Taste test.

5. When serving add dollop of sour cream and garnish with chopped parsley.

It's fun to serve this soup in a fresh pumpkin tureen. Fill a cleaned pumpkin with boiling water, put the lid on and let it set for ½ hour. Empty out water and pour in soup. Soup stays warm in the pumpkin.

108

Red Pepper Fish Chowder
Serves four to six

4	tbsp. butter
1	tbsp. lemon juice
2	medium onions, chopped
½	lb. mushrooms, chopped
2	red bell peppers, chopped
2	14 oz. cans chicken broth
1	lb. new potatoes, diced
2	tbsp. cornstarch
2	tbsp. water
1	cup sour cream
1½ -2	lb. firm white fish, cut into chunks
½	cup parsley
	salt to taste

1.   In large pot melt butter; add lemon juice, onions, mushrooms, and red peppers. Sauté until vegetables are tender. Add chicken broth and potatoes, cover and boil until potatoes are tender.

2. Blend cornstarch and water (Corn starch should have no lumps.) Stir into sour cream. Add cornstarch mixture a little at a time to soup liquid. Add fish and parsley. Simmer for 5 minutes, covered. Taste for seasoning as it may need a little more salt.

This is our family's favorite for Christmas Eve.

Russian Cabbage Soup
Serves four to six

8	cups beef stock
1	lb. kielbasa or turkey kielbasa cut into ¼" slices
1½	cups onions, chopped
1	cup carrots, chopped
2	cups celery, chopped
1	tsp. dill weed
2	tbsp. dried parsley flakes
2	cups tomatoes, chopped
2	cups potatoes, diced
1	lb. cabbage coarsely chopped (discard hard ribs and core)
	black pepper to taste

Garnish

regular or non-fat sour cream

1. Add beef stock to 6 quart stock pot and bring to simmer. In a sauté pan, sauté kielbasa, onion, carrots and potatoes. Add to stock along with the celery, dill weed, parsley, tomatoes, and ½ chopped cabbage. Simmer for one hour. Add reserved cabbage, bring to a boil and reduce heat, simmer 4 to 5 minutes.

2. Serve while very hot. If desired stir sour cream in soup.

Timothy's White Chili

Serves eight to ten

1	lb. northern white beans
1	tbsp. olive oil
2	lbs. boneless chicken breast cut into small pieces
2	medium onions, chopped
4	garlic cloves, diced
2	tsp. cumin
1½	tsp. oregano
¼	tsp. cayenne pepper
¼	tsp. ground cloves
1	7½ oz. can mild green chilies, chopped
2	cups jack cheese, grated
6	cups chicken broth

Garnish

salsa, sour cream and cilantro

1. Soak beans overnight and drain well.

2. In sauce pan cook chicken in oil. Remove and sauté onions and garlic in same pan.

3. In large Dutch oven or similar size pan, add broth, onion, garlic, drained beans and chicken pieces.

4. Add the spices: cumin, oregano, cayenne, cloves and green chilies. Simmer for 2 hours and add 1 cup of jack cheese.

5. Spoon into individual bowls and garnish with salsa, sour cream, cilantro and remaining cheese.

111

Tomato Bisque
Serves eight

½	cup butter
1	cup celery, chopped
1	cup onion, chopped
¼	cup carrots, chopped
⅓	cup flour
4	cups chicken stock
6	large fresh tomatoes peeled and chopped or 2 one pound twelve ounces cans of whole tomatoes
2	tsp. sugar
1	tsp. dried or fresh basil
1	tsp. dried marjoram
1	bay leaf
2	cups heavy cream
¼	tsp. paprika
¼	tsp. freshly ground white pepper
¼	tsp.curry powder
	salt and pepper to taste
1	roasting chicken cut into small pieces or shrimp

1. Melt butter in a large pan. Sauté celery, onions and carrots until tender. Add flour and cook for 2 minutes stirring constantly.

2. Add chicken stock and blend well. Add tomatoes, sugar, basil, marjoram and bay leaf. Cover and simmer for 30 minutes. Stir occasionally.

3. Discard bay leaf. In blender, puree one-third of mixture at a time until contents have been liqufied.

4. Return mixture to pot and add cream, paprika, and curry powder. Add roasted chicken or shrimp. Stir to blend and salt and pepper to taste.

5. Serve soup hot or cold. Refrigerate 3 to 4 hours or overnight. Garnish with a dollop of sour cream and chopped chives or garlic croutons.

Zesty Spinach Lentil Soup
Serves four

1	tsp. olive oil
1	cup red onion, finely chopped
½	cup dry lentils
5	cups chicken broth
2	tbsp. tomato paste
	dash cloves, ground
	freshly ground black pepper
2	cups fresh spinach, tightly packed and slivered

1. In stock pot over medium high heat, heat olive oil and sauté onion for 10 minutes. Add lentils, chicken broth, tomato paste and cloves. Season with pepper to taste. Slowly bring the soup to a boil, cover and simmer for 30 to 45 minutes, until lentils are soft.

2. Ladle hot soup over ½ cup spinach in individual soup bowls.

Zucchini Tomato Soup

Serves eight

4	medium size zucchini, sliced
5	tomatoes chopped
2	sweet yellow onions, sliced (4" diameter)
¼	cup butter
1½	cup dry white wine
2	garlic cloves, minced
2	tsp. basil leaf, chopped
1	bay leaf (remove after cooking and before serving)
1	cup jack cheese, grated
1	cup Romano cheese, grated
1	cup half and half

Preheat oven to 400°.

1. Toss and mix first 8 ingredients in heavy bake proof pot.

2. Bake for one hour.

3. Add cheeses and half and half. Stir until melted and serve.

This is a tasty summer soup, and a wonderful recipe for all the extra zucchini from your garden. It freezes well.

Helen Palmer lived near the Nez Perce Reservation in Lapwai; she is modeling a traditional dress lent to her by a close friend. She came to Sandpoint in 1924 and taught at Sunnyside with 9 students. Her teaching career included Lapwai, Sunnyside, Oden, Kootenai and Sandpoint. Reminiscing her life she mentioned that she came from the horseback days into the space age. On her 100th birthday one of her students presented her with a hug and an apple.

Scotchman Peak
Philip Hough

Salads

Sandpoint Women's Basketball Team 1910-1911
(L to R) Margery Catlin, Edith Bodgrey Phalon, Francis Page

Vivian Allen and Maude Hiner. Bonner County Historical Society Collection

Albeni Club Salad Dressing

1	cup vinegar
¾	cup sugar
1	cup salad oil
1	cup catsup
	dash paprika
1	tsp.Worcestershire sauce
1	tsp.prepared mustard
2	cloves of garlic, crushed
½	tsp. salt
	dash pepper

1. Measure the sugar and vinegar into a quart jar.

2. Stir well and add remaining ingredients.

3. Shake until it thickens.

4. Serve with any type of green salad

Apricot Mold
Serves ten

2	envelopes unflavored gelatin
1	cup cold water
1	cup apricot nectar
½	cup sugar
¼	tsp. salt
1	cup Chablis or other dry white wine
1	cup sour cream
1	17 oz. can apricot halves in heavy syrup, drained and chopped

Garnishes

Apricot halves and pecans

1. Sprinkle gelatin over cold water in a saucepan; let stand one minute. Add apricot nectar, sugar and salt. Cook over low heat stirring until gelatin and sugar dissolve.

2. Remove from heat. Add wine and sour cream; stir well. Fold in chopped apricots. Pour into oiled 5½ cup mold. Cover and chill until firm.

3. Unmold onto serving plate. Garnish and serve.

Avocado with Shrimp

Serves four to six

½	lb. small, cooked shrimp
2	hardboiled eggs, peeled
2	large or 3 small ripe avocados
1	tbsp. green onion, chopped
2	tbsp. fresh chives, chopped
¾-1	cup mayonnaise
2	tsp. tomato paste
	salt and pepper to taste
2	tsp. freshly squeezed lemon juice
	chopped chives or red pepper for garnish

1. Chop shrimp and eggs, not too finely, and place in a mixing bowl.

2. Cut avocados in half, remove pits. Scrape out pulp. Reserve shells. Dice pulp and add to shrimp.

3. Add chopped onion, chives, salt and pepper and mayonnaise. Mix well.

4. Add tomato paste for color. Taste and adjust seasonings. Fill avocado half shells and chill until ready to serve.

5. Before serving sprinkle lemon juice over the top for a flavor boost. Top with finely chopped chives or red pepper and serve.

Black Bean Salad
Serves six

2	15 oz. cans black beans, rinsed and drained
1	large red or yellow bell pepper, chopped
6	oz. feta cheese, crumbled
1	small red onion, chopped
1	10 oz. pkg. tiny frozen peas
1	head red leaf lettuce, separated

Salad Dressing

⅓	cup mayonnaise
⅓	cup sour cream
2	tbsp. balsamic vinegar
2	tbsp. applesauce
1	tbsp. olive oil
1	tbsp.Dijon mustard
1	tbsp. fresh dill
1	tsp. sugar

1. Mix dressing ingredients and blend until smooth.

2. Combine beans, pepper, cheese, onion and peas.

3. Add dressing and mix.

4. May top with chopped red and yellow peppers, or fresh cilantro, jicama or water chestnuts.

Serve on lettuce leaves.

This salad can be chilled all day or just mixed and served. The peas will thaw before they get to the table.

123

Ruthe (Mrs. Charles) Bond, circa 1930 at the Lawrence Moon cabin on Bottle Bay Road.

Bluegrass Salad
Serves six to eight

½	cup vegetable oil
¼	cup rice vinegar
1	tbsp. balsamic vinegar
2	tbsp. sugar
1	tsp. butter or margarine
¾	cup walnuts
2	heads romaine lettuce, torn
2	pears, chopped
1	cup asparagus tips*
½	cup dried cranberries
½	cup crumbled blue cheese

1. Whisk together the first four ingredients.

2. Chill at least 1 hour.

3. Melt butter in a skillet over medium heat. Add walnuts and sauté 5 minutes or until lightly browned. Remove walnuts with a slotted spoon.

4. Toss together lettuce, pears, asparagus and toasted walnuts. Sprinkle with cheese and cranberries; drizzle with dressing.

*One cup broccoli florets or one cup snow peas may be substituted for asparagus tips.

This elegant salad is different, delicious and light.

125

Broccoli Grape Salad

Serves six

Salad

4	cups small broccoli florets
2	cups red grapes cut in half
½	cup chopped red or sweet onion
½	lb. bacon, cooked and crumbled
1	large carrot, grated
½	cup sunflower seeds

Dressing

⅓	cup mayonnaise
2	tbsp. vinegar
3	tbsp. sugar
	salt and pepper to taste

1. Mix salad ingredients together in a salad bowl. Toss with ⅓ cup of dressing.

2. Refrigerate for at least 1 hour.

This is easy to make, yet elegant. Ideal salad for summer picnics and potlucks with grilled chicken or pork.

California Marinated Salad

Serves eight to ten

2	medium nectarines, sliced
½	lb. fresh mushrooms, quartered
1	cup cherry tomatoes, halved
½	cup pitted ripe olives
⅓	cup sliced scallions
1	6.5 oz. jar marinated artichoke hearts halved and quartered (drain and save marinade)

Salad Dressing

⅓	cup marinade from the artichoke jar plus vegetable oil, if needed
¼	cup lemon juice
¼	tsp. salt
¼	tsp. pepper
1	tsp. sugar
1	tsp. tarragon leaves
½	tsp. thyme

1. Combine salad ingredients in large bowl.

2. Mix dressing ingredients, shake and pour over salad.

3. Chill several hours, stirring occasionally.

The Pend D' Oreille, circa 1900
Owned by the Humbird Lumber Company
Jim Parsons Jr. Collection

Chicken Nectarine Salad
Serves six

4	boneless skinless chicken breasts

Marinade

4	tsp. lime juice
1½	tsp. olive oil
2	tsp. thyme
1	tsp. minced garlic

Salad

5	nectarines peeled and sliced
6	cups salad greens
1	tsp. pine nuts, toasted
½	cup fresh raspberries

Dressing

3	tbsp. lime juice
1	tbsp. thyme
1	tbsp. olive oil
	dash garlic powder

1. Mix marinade ingredients. Put chicken breasts in a large zip lock bag and pour in marinade. Marinate for 1 to 4 hours, turning bag occasionally.

2. Grill chicken. Discard the marinade.

3. Mix salad ingredients and dressing ingredients.

4. Slice grilled chicken and add to salad mixture. Drizzle dressing over the top and serve.

129

Chicken Potato Salad
Serves six

3	boneless, skinless chicken breasts, cooked
1	lb. small new potatoes, cooked with skins on
1	red bell pepper, seeded and cut into strips
3	green onions, chopped

Dressing

½	cup fresh basil leaves
2	cloves garlic, minced
3	tbsp. grated Parmesan cheese
½	tsp. oregano
¼	cup white wine vinegar
½	cup extra virgin olive oil
	salt and pepper

1. Cut potatoes and chicken into 1 inch pieces. Toss with red pepper and green onions.

2. Mix remaining ingredients in a food processor and pureé. Toss with chicken-potato mixture.

Try this for buffets, picnics or potlucks

Crab and Shrimp Salad

1	20 oz. package frozen peas
½	lb. shelled crab
½	lb. cooked shrimp
2	cups chopped celery
¾	cup mayonnaise
1	tbsp. lemon juice
2	tbsp. chili sauce
½	tsp. curry powder
	garlic salt to taste
½	cup roasted cashews
1	pkg. fine chow mein noodles
1	head of lettuce

1. Thaw peas and combine all ingredients except cashews, chow mein noodles and lettuce.

2. Mix well, and chill several hours to overnight.

3. Just before serving add nuts. Serve on a bed of lettuce and top with chow mein noodles.

Green onions are also good in this.

Cranberry Walnut Salad
Serves six

12	oz. baby greens
½	red onion, thinly sliced
4	oz. Gorgonzola cheese, crumbled
4	oz. dried cranberries
4	oz. caramelized walnuts

Dressing

1	tbsp. crushed garlic
1	tbsp. Dijon mustard
½	tsp. salt and pepper
1	tbsp. lemon juice
¼	cup white wine vinegar
½	cup olive oil

Caramelized walnuts

1	lb.walnuts
¾	cup water
1	cup sugar
1	tbsp. vanilla

1. Combine dressing ingredients and mix well.

2. To caramelize walnuts heat together water, sugar, vanilla and walnuts on low heat. Cook down liquid stirring it every few minutes. It will take about 30 minutes. (Recipe will produce more walnuts than needed; store in an airtight container.)

3. Put salad ingredients in bowl. Add dressing and toss.

Farfalle and Spinach Salad

Serves six to eight

Salad

1½	bags fresh spinach
16	oz. farfalle pasta, cooked al dente, drained
1	8 oz. bag dried cranberries
3	11 oz. cans Mandarin oranges, drained
2	8 oz. cans water chestnuts, drained
½	cup chopped parsley
1	bunch green onions, chopped
¼	cup sesame seeds, toasted
6	oz. honey-roasted peanuts
1	lb. cooked skinless, boneless chicken breast pieces, sliced ¼" thick

Dressing

1	cup olive oil
⅔	cup teriyaki sauce
⅓	cup white wine vinegar
6	tbsp. sugar
½	tsp. salt
½	tsp. pepper

1. Combine all dressing ingredients and mix well. Marinate cooked farfalle pasta in half the dressing for several hours.

2. Toss all ingredients together along with rest of dressing and serve.

Hot Plum & Spinach Salad
Serves six to eight

4	slices thick cut bacon
8	cups baby spinach
½	lb. red skin plums, pitted and halved
4	tsp. coarse grain Dijon mustard
2	tbsp. red wine vinegar
1	tsp. sugar

1. Fry bacon, cut into small pieces and drain on paper towel. Reserve 2 tablespoons drippings.

2. Heat drippings on high. Add mustard, vinegar and sugar, and stir. Add plums; heat to boil.

3. Pour plum mixture over spinach. Sprinkle with bacon. Serve immediately.

Hot Plum and Spinach Salad is a wonderful choice when looking for a sweet salad.

Indonesian Rice Salad

Serves six to eight

2	cups cooked basmati brown rice
½	cup raisins
2	green onions, chopped
¼	cup toasted sesame seeds
½	cup thinly sliced water chestnuts
1	cup fresh bean sprouts
¼	cup toasted cashews
1	green pepper, chopped
1	stalk celery, chopped
	freshly chopped parsley
	salt and pepper to taste
	leaf lettuce

Dressing

⅔	cup orange juice
⅓	cup olive oil
	juice of 1 lemon
3-4	tbsp. soy sauce
2	tbsp. dry sherry
1	clove garlic, minced
1	tsp. freshly grated ginger root

1. Place all salad ingredients except lettuce leaves in large bowl. Season with salt and pepper.

2. Mix dressing ingredients together. Toss salad with dressing. Chill until ready to serve. Arrange lettuce leaves on platter; spoon salad on lettuce leaves.

135

Mango Beet Salad
Serves Six

2   lbs. beets, cooked
1   ripe mango, peeled
¼   cup rice vinegar
¼   tsp. coarse salt
⅓   tsp. freshly ground pepper
      pinch sugar

1. Slice beets very thin. Cube mango.

2. Whisk together vinegar, salt, pepper and sugar.

3. Put beets and mango on a bed of greens and drizzle on dressing. Serve.

This is a beautiful and very refreshing salad.

Mexican Cucumber Salad
Serves four to six

3	cucumbers, peeled and chopped
1	medium sweet onion, chopped fairly fine
2	jalapeno chilies, chopped fine or to taste
3	tbsp. fresh lime juice
¼	tsp. coarse kosher salt
¼	cup chopped cilantro

Mix all ingredients together in a bowl. For best results, use exact amounts of lime juice and cilantro. Serve.

This easy and refreshing summer salad is wonderful with grilled fish.

Pasta Salad with Spinach and Feta Cheese

Serves six to eight

½   lb. shells or bow pasta
1   lb. fresh spinach
2   tomatoes, chopped
½   bunch scallions, finely chopped
1   cucumber peeled and thinly sliced
½   cup feta cheese, crumbled
½   cup pine nuts, toasted

Dressing

⅓   cup olive oil
⅓   cup champagne vinegar
2   cloves garlic, minced
1   tsp. Dijon mustard
¼   cup freshly grated Parmesan cheese
½   tsp. dried oregano
      salt and pepper to taste

1. Combine dressing ingredients and blend well.

2. Cook pasta until tender. Drain and toss with half of the dressing.

3. Trim stems from spinach and shred.

4. Combine all salad ingredients in large bowl. Toss with remainder of dressing.

5. Serve fresh or refrigerate for later use.

Rice, Black Bean and Feta Salad
Serves five

1	15-oz. can black beans, rinsed and drained
1½	cups chopped tomatoes
1½	cups cooked rice
4	oz. crumbled feta cheese (variation: Garlic and Herb Feta Cheese)
½	cup chopped celery
½	cup chopped green onions
½	cup Italian dressing
2	tbsp. chopped fresh cilantro (or parsley)
1	clove garlic, minced

Mix all ingredients, refrigerate and serve.

This hearty summer salad can be served as a main course or a side dish with chicken or fish.

Rice or Penne Pasta Salad
Serves ten

2	cups long-grain rice or ½ box penne pasta
4	cups water
1½	tsp. salt
2	bay leaves
1	tbsp. plus 1 tsp. olive oil
½	cup pine nuts, toasted
½	lb. mushrooms, quartered
¾	lb. shrimp, peeled and deveined
⅓	cup drained capers
3	tbsp. fresh chives
⅓	cup cooked peas

Dressing

2	tbsp. fresh lemon juice
2	tbsp. balsamic vinegar
1	tbsp. Dijon mustard
1	tbsp. minced shallot or red onion
¾	tsp. salt
4	dashes of Tabasco
2	tsp. dried oregano or 2 tbsp. fresh
⅓	cup olive oil

1. Boil pasta in water and salt or cook rice with bay leaves. Discard bay leaves.

2. Sauté pine nuts in 1 teaspoon olive oil until light brown. Dry on a paper towel.

3. Sauté shrimp and mushrooms in 1 tablespoon olive oil for 2-3 minutes. (Be careful not to over cook.)

4. Place all dressing ingredients except oil in blender; add olive oil while blender is running.

5. Put all salad ingredients in large bowl and lightly toss. Pour on dressing a little at a time and toss; taste test as you add. Serve with extra dressing.

Salad absorbs dressing over time so go easy when first adding dressing. An assortment of grilled vegetables can be added to this versatile salad.

circa 1930
Jim Parsons Jr. Collection

Roast Beef Salad

Serves eight

Salad

1	two lb. beef roast cooked rare, cooled, and sliced thinly
1	8 oz. can whole beets, drained, cut into julienne strips
4	large shallots, minced
¾	lb. fresh snow peas
¼	cup fresh parsley, chopped
	salad greens

Dressing

⅓	cup balsamic vinegar
⅔	cup olive oil
1	tbsp. Dijon mustard

1. Combine roast beef, beets and shallots in large bowl. Add vinaigrette and mix to coat beef. Refrigerate covered for one hour.

2. Meanwhile, cook peas in boiling, salted water for 2 minutes. Drain, and rinse in cold water. Refrigerate.

3. Add peas to roast beef mixture and mix well. Place in serving bowl. Sprinkle with parsley, and season with salt and pepper.

4. Refrigerate covered for two hours or overnight.

5. Serve cold on a bed of greens.

143

Shallot Dessing

¾   cup light oil
¼   cup tarragon wine vinegar
3   shallots, finely chopped
1   tbsp. fresh parsley, minced
1   clove garlic, minced
2   tsp. Dijon mustard
½   tsp. salt
½   tsp. ground pepper

1. Combine all ingredients except oil.

2. Whisk oil into ingredients.

Can be refrigerated up to two weeks.

Spinach Salad
Serves six to eight

Salad

10   oz. fresh spinach
½   cup slivered almonds, toasted
¼   cup sunflower seeds
½-1   cup garlic croutons
2–3   slices bacon, cooked, crumbled
1   apple, diced
¼   cup green onions, chopped
½   cup mushrooms, sliced

Honey Salad Dressing

2   tbsp. sugar
1   tsp. dry mustard
1   tsp. paprika
1   tsp. celery seed
¼   tsp. salt
1   tsp. grated onion
⅓   cup honey
5   tbsp. white vinegar
1   tbsp. freshly squeezed lemon juice
¼   tsp. salt
1   cup salad oil

1. Mix dry ingredients; add onion, honey, vinegar and lemon juice. Pour oil in slowly, beating continually. A blender or food processor works well.

2. Add ½ cup dressing or to taste. Toss and serve.

Strawberry Spinach Salad

Serves four to six

Salad

1½	lbs. fresh spinach
1	pint fresh strawberries, sliced
3	tbsp. sesame seeds, toasted

Dressing

¾	cup honey
2	tsp. Dijon mustard
½	cup balsamic vinegar
	salt and pepper to taste

1. Mix dressing ingredients.

2. Mix spinach and strawberries together in large salad bowl.

3. Add dressing and toss.

4. Mix in sesame seeds.

Reserve a few whole strawberries and sesame seeds for garnish.

Stuffed Lettuce

2-4	oz. blue cheese
1	3 oz. pkg. cream cheese
2	tbsp. mayonnaise
1	tbsp. cream
1	tbsp. chopped green onion
1	tbsp. chopped parsley
1	tbsp. pimiento, optional
1	head iceburg lettuce

1. Blend blue cheese, cream cheese, mayonnaise, cream, green onion, parsley and pimiento together in food processor.

2. Remove inside core of head lettuce leaving an inch of lettuce.

3. Stuff the hole with dressing.

4. Refrigerate overnight or for 8 hours.

Cut into wedges and serve.

Summer Salad

Serves four

2 cups fresh beet greens
2 tsp. fresh chives
½ cup cooked broccoli flowerets
1 tbsp. fresh minced basil
  balsamic dressing to taste

1. Tear up beet greens, avoiding tough, red stems. Mix with chives, cooled broccoli flowerets and fresh minced basil.

2. Toss with balsamic dressing and serve immediately.

Thai Shrimp Salad
Serves six

1½	fresh papaya, cubed
1	large red bell pepper, sliced, cut in triangles
1	cucumber, diced
1	lb. cooked fresh shrimp
½	cup toasted pine nuts

Dressing

3	tbsp. lime juice
2	tbsp. brown sugar
2	tsp. fish sauce
1	tbsp. finely chopped ginger
3	tbsp. chopped cilantro
1	tsp. Chinese chili sauce

1. Cut papaya, pepper and cucumber; mix with shrimp in large bowl.

2. Mix ingredients for dressing and pour over salad. Sprinkle with pine nuts.

3. Serve immediately or chill. For chilled salad, make dressing the night before. Assemble salad, add dressing and chill 2 hours. Sprinkle pine nuts at serving time.

Tomato Basil Summer Salad

Serves four to six

4-6	ripe red tomatoes
3-4	balls of fresh mozzarella, 4 oz. size
½	cup slivered basil
⅓	cup toasted pine nuts
¼	cup balsamic vinegar

1. Slice tomatoes and mozzarella cheese.

2. Arrange the sliced tomatoes on a platter. Cover with thin mozzarella slices.

3. Sprinkle with fresh basil and top with toasted pine nuts.

4. Drizzle with balsamic vinegar and serve as an appetizer, salad or part of a salad buffet.

Tomato Artichoke Salad
Serves four

2   cups cherry tomatoes, cut in half
1   cup marinated artichoke hearts, quartered
⅓   cup pitted kalamata olives sliced
¼   cup chopped red or sweet onions
⅓   cup crumbled feta cheese
⅓   cup fresh basil leaves

Dressing

       dash dry mustard
1   tbsp. white balsamic vinegar
1½   cloves garlic, minced
1½   tbsp. water
¼   tsp. salt
       dash white pepper
1   tsp. sugar
1½   tbsp. olive oil

1. Combine dressing ingredients except oil; whisk in olive oil.

2. Combine salad ingredients except basil.

3. When ready to serve, add thinly sliced basil leaves to salad along with dressing, and toss.

151

Tropical Turkey Salad
Serves six to eight

1	lb. cooked turkey, cubed
4	stalks celery, sliced
1	16 oz. can pineapple chunks, drained
½	cup peanuts
½	cups raisins
2	green onions, chopped

Dressing

¾	cup mayonnaise
¼	cup apple butter
½	tsp. curry (optional)

1. Combine mayonnaise, apple butter and curry in a small bowl. Set Aside.

2. Mix together salad ingredients, add dressing and toss.

Sandpoint Marina
Foster Cline, MD.

Meat, Poultry
& Game

Meats, Poultry & Game

1939 Safeway Grand Opening (L to R) Al Madsen

BEEF
ROAST
18¢/lb

ARMOUR'S
PICNICS
15¢/lb

Boston
Buns
20¢/lb

Clover
20¢/lb

Sink
HAMS
25¢/lb

19¢/lb

8¢/lb

20¢/lb
18¢/lb

12¢/lb

23¢/lb

31¢/lb

28¢/lb

32¢

23

27

23

27

SHANKS POT ROAST

SHORT RIBS BONELESS BEEF STEW ROUND STEAK

SHORT RIBS PORK CHOPS VEAL STEAK VEAL ROUND

and Dick Clary. Bonner County Historical Society

Alsatian Pork Roast

Serves eight to ten

1	8 lb. pork loin roast
1	tsp. salt
½	tsp. pepper
1	tsp. marjoram
2	bay leaves

Sauce

¼	cup butter
6	shallots, thinly sliced
½	cup flour
2	cups dry white wine
1	lb. fresh mushrooms, sliced
2	Spanish onions, peeled and thinly sliced
1	cup sauerkraut with juice
1	cup sauerkraut without juice
2	cups sour cream
3-4	beef bouillon cubes
1	tbsp. chives
	salt and pepper to taste

Preheat oven to 500°.

1. Rub pork roast with salt, pepper and ½ tsp. marjoram. Place in roasting pan with bay leaves and roast uncovered for 20-30 minutes.

3. While meat is cooking make the sauce. In a 4 quart saucepan melt the butter until it sizzles. Brown shallots lightly, stir in flour and cook for 2 minutes. Add wine and mix thoroughly. Add mushrooms,

onions, sauerkraut and juice, sour cream, bouillon cubes, chives, and remaining majoram. Blend well. Add salt and pepper to taste.

4. Remove roast from oven and drain off fat. Reduce heat to 350°. Pour sauce over meat, cover and return to oven. Cook for 2½ - 3 hours (137° on a meat thermometer) until juices run clear when roast is pierced with a fork.

5. Let rest for about 15 minutes before slicing.

Berry Orange Relish
Serve with ham or turkey

1	large orange, quartered and seeded
1	12 oz. package cranberries
¾	cup sugar
2	tbsp. Grand Marnier or Triple Sec
1	6 oz. pkg. dry frozen raspberries

1. Blend all ingredients in a food processor, or coarsely hand chop fruit and mix all ingredients together.

2. Serve with ham or turkey.

3. Keeps well in the refrigerator.

Bistro Chicken

Serves four

4	chicken leg quarters
2	tbsp. chopped fresh basil (2 tsp. dried)
2	tbsp. chopped fresh thyme (2 tsp. dried)
2	tbsp. chopped fresh rosemary (2 tsp. dried, crushed)
2	cloves garlic, minced
4	tsp. olive oil
1	tsp. salt
½	tsp. ground black pepper

Preheat oven to 375°

1. Rinse chicken with cold water and pat dry.
Trim excess fat. Loosen skin from thigh and leg by inserting fingers, pushing gently between skin and meat.

2. Combine remaining ingredients. Rub herb mixture under skin.

3. Place chicken on broiler pan. Bake for 45 minutes. Increase oven temperature to 450°. (Do not remove chicken.) Bake 30 minutes more. Remove from oven; cover loosely with foil; let stand 10 minutes.

4. Discard skin before serving.

Bobotie

2	lbs. ground beef
2	onions, diced
1	slice bread
1	cup milk
2	eggs
1	tbsp. curry powder
1½	tsp. sugar
2	tsp. salt
½	tsp. pepper
½	tbsp. turmeric
2	tbsp. vinegar
6	quartered almonds
½	cup raisins
4	bay leaves
3	tbsp. chutney or 1 tbsp. apricot jam

Preheat oven to 350°.

1. Fry the onions, add ground beef and cook until browned.

2. Soak bread in milk; squeeze milk out; crumble bread.

3. Mix all ingredients except one egg, ½ cup milk and bay leaves.

4. Put the mixture in a baking dish and place bay leaves upright in the mixture. Bake for 1½ hours.

5. Beat remaining egg and milk. Pour over meat 30 minutes before it comes out of the oven. Serve with Yellow Raisin Rice, Currried Grape Chutney and sliced bananas.

Yellow Raisin Rice

1	cup rice
1	tsp. salt
3	cups water
1-1½	tsp. tumeric
	handful of raisins

Add rice and salt to water and cook until water is absorbed (20-25 minutes). Stir in turmeric and raisins until rice is an even yellow color.

Curried Grape Chutney

2½	lbs. onions, chopped
4	cups sugar
1	tbsp. salt
3	cups white vinegar
1	tbsp. cloves
2	tsp. coriander
2	tbsp. Wonderpepper (Beaumonde)
1	tbsp. chopped fresh ginger
5	lbs. seedless grapes
2	tbsp. curry powder
1	tsp. tumeric
1	tbsp. cornstarch

1. Boil onions, sugar and salt in vinegar for 10 minutes.

2. Add spices, except curry and turmeric, in garni bag. Boil until onions are soft. Add grapes. Boil 20 minutes. Mix curry, tumeric and corn starch with a bit of vinegar. Add and cook until thickened. Remove bag of spices. Cool and bottle.

Barbara Blood (Mrs. Irvin) moved to Sandpoint from Nebraska in 1939. She couldn't believe the abundance! They canned 1000 quarts of fruits and vegetables one fall.

Chicken Cacciatore

3	lbs. cubed boneless, skinned chicken, breast or thighs
3	tbsp. olive oil
2	medium onions, sliced thinly
2	cloves garlic, minced
1	lb. canned tomatoes
1	8 oz. can tomato sauce
	green pepper, thinly sliced
1	tsp. salt
¼	tsp. pepper
¼	tsp. cayenne pepper
1	tsp. dried oregano
½	tsp. crushed basil
½	tsp. celery salt
1	bay leaf
¼	cup Chianti wine
	buttered pasta

Preheat oven to 325°.

1. Brown chicken pieces in olive oil. Place onion on the bottom of a large casserole and top with the chicken.

2. Combine all other ingredients and pour on top of chicken. Bake for 1 hour. Discard bay leaf.

3. Spoon chicken and sauce over buttered pasta before serving.

Chicken Parmesan with Sicilian Tomato Sauce

Serves six

6	boneless, skinless chicken breasts
1	tbsp. olive oil
1½	cups Sicilian Tomato Sauce
⅓	cup whipping cream
⅓	lb. mozzarella cheese, grated
¼	cup grated Parmesan cheese
½	tsp. dried marjoram
	salt and pepper to taste

Preheat oven to 350°.

1. Season chicken with salt and pepper. Heat a large nonstick frying pan and add the oil. Brown chicken lightly on both sides and remove.

2. Combine Sicilian Tomato Sauce with cream and pour ½ cup into a 9" x 13" baking dish.

3. Arrange chicken over sauce and add remaining sauce. Cover chicken with mozzarella and Parmesan cheeses. Sprinkle with marjoram.

4. Bake for about 20 minutes or until brown.

Fresh Sicilian Tomato Sauce
Makes about 10 pints

¼	cup olive oil
4	cloves garlic, crushed
1	medium onion, finely chopped
9	cups cored and chopped very ripe tomatoes
4	28 oz. cans whole tomatoes crushed with juice
¼	cup chopped parsley
½	cup dry white wine
1	cup chicken stock
1	tsp. dried marjoram
1	tsp. dried rosemary
6	tbsp. butter
	salt and pepper to taste

1. Heat a large heavy-bottomed pot. Add oil, garlic and onion. Sauté until onions are clear.

2. Add remaining ingredients except for butter, salt and pepper.

3. Bring to a simmer and gently cook uncovered for four hours. Stir often.

4. Stir in butter, salt and pepper.

Citrus Roasted Chicken
Serves four

1	3 lb. chicken
2	lemons
2	oranges
	fresh thyme sprigs
2	cloves elephant garlic
½	cup white wine
	salt and pepper

Preheat oven to 425°.

1. Rinse chicken in cold water inside and out. Dry and add salt and pepper.

2. Cut 1 lemon, 1 orange and 2 cloves of garlic into chunks. Add to cavity with sprigs of fresh thyme. Truss chicken. Insert thyme sprigs under chicken skin at breast.

3. Roast for 15 minutes.

4. Juice remaining lemon and orange and add wine. Reduce heat to 350° and baste chicken with citrus juices and wine. Roast 1½ hours.

Goes well with garlic or wild mushroom couscous (add a little white wine) or wild rice.

Crisp Baked Chicken
Serves four

4	lbs. chicken pieces including legs, thighs and wings
8	slices day-old white bread
2¼	oz. Parmesan cheese finely grated
1	tbsp. chopped fresh rosemary
¾	tsp. freshly ground pepper
1	cup buttermilk
1	tsp. Tabasco sauce
¾	tsp. coarse salt
	parchment paper

Preheat over to 400°.

1. Line baking sheet with parchment paper.

2. In a food processor grind bread into fine crumbs.

3. In a shallow bowl combine bread crumbs, Parmesan, rosemary and ¼ tsp. pepper.

4. In another bowl combine buttermilk, Tabasco, salt and remaining pepper.

5. Dip each of chicken pieces into liquid mixture then into bread crumb mixture. Turn and coat all sides and place each on baking sheet.

6. Bake for 40 minutes. Rotate pan halfway through cooking.

Chinese BBQ Flank Steak
Serves two to four

1   1½ lb. flank steak

Marinade

4   tbsp. soy sauce
1   tbsp. sherry
1   tsp. brown sugar
1   tsp. grated fresh ginger (Don't substitute dry ginger.)
1   clove garlic, smashed
1   tsp. Hoisin Sauce (Find in Chinese section of grocery store.)
2   green onions, finely chopped

1. Combine all ingredients for marinade. Pour over flank steak and marinate for 3 to 4 hours in a plastic bag, turning several times.

2. Barbeque on very hot charcoal fire until done, about 6 minutes on each side.

3. Slice across grain into thin slices and serve.

Irma, Mae, John and Gloria Tillburg, 1934.
Mae Burt Collection

Fruited Pot Roast

Serves six to eight

1   3-4 lb. pot roast

Marinade

12   oz. mixed dried fruit (apricots, pitted prunes, pears, plums, cranberries)
16   oz. beer
1   large onion, chopped
½   cup water
1   clove garlic, minced
¼   cup brown sugar
1   bay leaf
1   tsp. minced fresh parsley
¼   tsp. cinnamon
1½   tsp. salt
¼   tsp. freshly ground pepper

1. Mix marinade in a large bowl. Place roast in pan and cover with marinade. Marinate for several hours or overnight.

2. Remove pot roast from marinade and brown in a roasting pan. Reserve marinade.

3. Pour marinade back over roast and cover. Cook in 275° oven for about 4 hours.

4. Place roast on a platter and surround with fruit and sauce. Serve with buttered noodles or rice.

Greek Ragu
Serves eight

3	lbs. beef chuck, trimmed of fat and cut into 1½ inch cubes
	salt and ground pepper
½	cup butter
2½	lbs. small white onions, peeled and coarsely chopped
1	6 oz. can tomato paste
⅔	cup red wine
2	tbsp. red wine vinegar
1	tbsp. light brown sugar
1	clove garlic, finely chopped
1	whole bay leaf
1	small cinnamon stick
½	tsp. whole cloves
½	tsp. ground cumin
2	tbsp. dried currants or raisins

1. In large bowl, place meat and season with salt and pepper. In a heavy kettle, over low heat, melt butter. Add meat and stir to coat with butter, but do not let brown. Place onions on top of the meat.

2. In small bowl, blend tomato paste, wine, vinegar, sugar, and garlic and pour over the beef-onion mixture. Add bay leaf, cinnamon stick, cloves, cumin and currants or raisins. Cover kettle with lid and simmer for three hours. Meat will be very tender.

3. Spoon over buttered noodles and serve.

Gourmet Meatloaf

Serves eight

1	lb. hot Italian sausage
2	lbs. ground chuck
1	medium onion, chopped
4	cloves garlic, finely chopped
1⅓	cups dry bread crumbs
1	cup chopped Italian parsley
2	eggs, beaten
½	cup tomato sauce
½	cup red wine
1	tsp. dried oregano
1	tsp. salt
1	tsp. pepper
2¼	cups chopped fresh spinach
4	oz. oil-packed sun-dried tomatoes, drained
⅓	cup chopped black olives
1	lb. mozzarella cheese, thinly sliced

Preheat oven to 350°.

1. Remove sausage from casings and crumble. In a bowl, combine sausage with ground chuck, onion, garlic, bread crumbs, parsley, eggs, tomato sauce, wine, oregano, salt and pepper. Mix well.

2. Spread mixture into a large rectangular pan (12" x 15") lined with waxed paper (leave hanging over sides to grab).

3. Spread spinach over the middle of this mixture, leaving edges uncovered. Cover spinach layer with tomatoes, olives and ¾ of cheese.

4. Roll the meat loaf into a log, using wax paper to begin the roll. Remove the waxed paper; press the edges to seal and place seam side down in a foil-lined baking pan.

5. Bake for about 1 hour until cooked through.

6. Top with remaining cheese and put back in the oven just long enough to melt cheese.

Serve hot or cold. Good with garlicky mashed potatoes and green salad.

Greek Meatball Pitas
Serves four

½   lb. lean ground lamb
2   tbsp. finely chopped onion
¼   tsp. salt
½   tsp. dried oregano
½   tsp. minced garlic
¼   tsp. black pepper

Sauce

½   cup plain low fat yogurt
½   cup diced cucumber
2   tsp. finely chopped onion
¾   tsp. dried dill
½   tsp. sugar

Pita

2   cups salad greens
8   slices plum tomatoes
2   six-inch pitas cut in half

Preheat oven to 450°.

1. Combine the first 6 ingredients.

2. Shape mixture into sixteen 1" meatballs and flatten. Place on broiler pan and bake for 12 minutes or until done.

4. Mix together sauce ingredients.

5. Arrange four meatballs, ½ cup greens and two tomato slices in each pita half. Drizzle each with ¼ cup sauce.

Early 1900s Renovation
Jim Parsons Jr. Collection

"The Nettleingham Sisters"
Mabel Selberg and Mahala Timblin
Robert Gunter Collection

Leg of Lamb
Serves eight

1   leg of lamb butterflied, defatted and deboned

Marinade

2   cloves garlic, crushed
⅔   cup canola oil
¼   cup lemon juice or red wine vinegar
½   cup chopped onions
1   tbsp. Dijon mustard
2   tsp. kosher salt
1   tsp. oregano
1   tsp. basil
     pepper to taste
1   bay leaf, crushed
     crushed mint leaves

1. Mix together marinade ingredients and marinate lamb overnight.

2. Broil lamb over hot coals for 45 minutes to one hour. Meat should be charred outside and pink inside.

Marinated Filet of Beef

1	5-6 lb. filet of beef
4-5	garlic cloves, slivered
1	tsp. salt
1	tsp. freshly ground pepper
½	tsp. Tabasco sauce
1	cup soy sauce
½	cup olive oil
1¼	inch piece of ginger root, peeled and grated
1	cup port wine
1	tsp. thyme
1	bay leaf
	bacon strips to cover the top

1. Make small gashes in beef and push in slivers of garlic.

2. Rub roast well with salt, pepper and Tabasco sauce.

3. Combine soy sauce, oil, ginger root, port and herbs.

4. Place beef in a shallow dish and pour marinade over.

5. Cover and chill 3 hours or overnight. Turn several times.

6. Transfer beef to a rack in a shallow pan and cover with bacon strips. Save marinade. Roast at 425° for about 28 minutes for rare; 35 minutes for medium. Baste several times with marinade.

"Waiting for the Train," circa 1900s
Jim Parsons Jr. Collection

Oven Baked Ribs
Serves five to eight

2	tsp. Spike Seasoning
1	tsp. Accent Seasoning
½	tsp. fresh ground pepper
5	racks of baby back ribs (about 5 lbs.)
6	cloves garlic, minced
2	large jalapeño peppers, seeded and minced
2	large onions, thinly sliced
2	green bell peppers, thinly sliced
2	red bell peppers, thinly sliced
2	yellow bell peppers, thinly sliced

1. In cup combine Spike, Accent and pepper. Sprinkle ¼ tsp. mixture on each side of rib racks.

2. In small bowl combine garlic, jalapeño peppers and remaining 1 tsp. seasoning mixture. Rub mixture on top and bottom of ribs.

3. Line 17" x 12" roasting pan with enough foil to wrap all ribs.

4. Spread layer of onions and bell peppers on foil. Place two rib racks side-by-side on vegetables. Continue to layer onions, peppers, and ribs until you have used all of ribs. Tightly wrap ribs in foil and refrigerate for 2 days.

5. Remove pan from refrigerator and let sit at room

temperature for 30 minutes.

6. Preheat oven to 400°.

7. Before placing ribs in oven, reduce temperature to 300°. Bake foil-wrapped ribs for 6 to 8 hours.

8. Remove ribs; skim fat from liquid and discard. Reserve pan juices.

9. Cut racks into individual serving sizes and serve with vegetables and pan juices.

Pork Tenderloin with Honey Butter
Serves four

1	1½ lb. pork tenderloin
6	tbsp. butter
3	tbsp. honey
	fresh rosemary, chopped
	coarse salt and freshly ground pepper
⅓	cup water

Preheat oven to 375°.

1. In Dutch oven or ovenproof skillet, heat butter and honey over medium-low heat, stirring to melt butter.

2. Season pork to taste with salt and pepper and place in pan.

3. Cook until lightly browned on all sides, about 10 minutes. Reduce heat if honey begins to burn.

4. Sprinkle with rosemary. Transfer to oven and roast until pork is cooked to 145°, 12-15 minutes; transfer to a plate and cover with foil.

5. Add water to pan and place on stove over medium heat; cook, stirring to scrape up all browned bits. Add any accumulated pork juices from plate, and simmer until sauce is reduced to about ¾ cup.

6. Slice pork on the diagonal; drizzle with sauce and serve.

Pork Tenderloin with Peach Salsa
Serves eight

2	1 lb. pork tenderloins, trimmed
1	tbsp. ground cumin
1	tsp. salt
¼	tsp. ground cloves
¼	tsp. ground red pepper
¼	tsp. freshly ground pepper
	cooking oil spray

Peach Salsa

3½	cups diced, peeled peaches (2 ½ lbs.)
¼	cup diced red onion
2	tbsp. finely chopped fresh cilantro
1	tbsp. minced, seeded jalapeno pepper
2	tbsp. rice vinegar
1	tsp. fresh lemon juice
1	clove garlic, minced

Preheat oven to 375°.

1. Combine all salsa ingredients and mix well. Cover and chill.

2. Combine spices and rub pork with mixture. Place on broiler pan coated with cooking spray.

3. Bake 20 minutes or until meat thermometer registers 160°.

4. Slice pork and serve with peach salsa (serving size ¼ cup).

183

Best Friends, 1900s
Jim Parsons Jr. Collection

Rio Grande Pork Roast
Serves eight to ten

1	4-5 lb. boneless rolled pork loin roast
½	tsp. salt
½	tsp. garlic powder
1	tsp. chili powder
½	cup apple jelly
½	cup catsup
1	tbsp. vinegar or red wine
1	cup crushed corn chips

Preheat oven to 325°.

1. Place pork, fat side up, in a shallow roasting pan. Combine salt, garlic and ½ tsp. chili powder. Rub mixture into roast.

2. Roast for 2-2 ½ hours or until meat thermometer reads 165°.

3. Combine jelly, catsup, vinegar and remaining chili powder.

4. Bring to a boil and reduce heat. Simmer uncovered for about 2 minutes.

5. Brush roast with glaze. Sprinkle with corn chips and continue roasting for another 10 to 15 minutes, or until meat thermometer reads 170°.

6. Remove from oven and let rest for 10 minutes.

Serve with beans and rice, sliced avocados and tortillas.

185

Roasted Haunch of Venison

1   6-7 lb. venison roast

Marinade

5   tbsp. butter
1   large onion, chopped
2   tbsp. chopped green onion
2   large carrots, chopped
4   whole cloves
½   tsp. thyme
½   tsp. marjoram
½   tsp. tarragon
½   tsp.basil
½   tsp. rosemary
½   tsp. mustard seeds
2   cups dry red wine
      olive oil
      salt and freshly ground pepper
½   lb. salt pork
2   cloves garlic, slivered

Gravy

1   cup red currant jelly
      pinch powdered ginger
      pinch powdered cloves
1   tsp. lemon juice
¼   cup sour cream
      flour (if necessary for thickening)
1   tbsp. brandy

1. Prepare marinade by browning onions and carrots in butter.

2. Add cloves, thyme, marjoram, tarragon, basil, rosemary, and mustard seeds.

3.   Add 1 cup of red wine and put everything through a coarse sieve.

4. Brush venison with olive oil; dust with plenty of salt and freshly ground pepper.

5. Pour marinade over venison and let it marinate for about 8 hours. Reserve marinade.

6. Lard venison generously with salt pork.

7. Insert garlic slivers into slits made in top of roast.

8. Roast in 450° oven 20 to 30 minutes for each pound. Baste frequently with drippings and reserved marinade. When meat is tender remove from roasting pan. Keep meat warm while preparing gravy.

Gravy

1. In roasting pan melt jelly with drippings and marinade. Add remaining cup of red wine, ginger, cloves, and lemon juice.

2. When gravy is thickened and reduced a little, slowly add sour cream and blend everything thoroughly.

3. For thicker gravy sprinkle a little flour on top and stir in thoroughly making certain no lumps form. Just before serving add brandy and pour the gravy into gravy boat.

Snow on the Mountain
Serves ten to twelve

3-4   cups cooked rice
2   whole chickens
1   onion, chopped
3   stalks celery, chopped
5   peppercorns
4   chicken bouillon cubes
4   tbsp. butter
4   tbsp. flour
      curry powder to taste

Condiments

      chopped tomatoes
      finely chopped onions
      Chinese noodles heated until crisp
      diagonally sliced celery
      black and green sliced olives
1   lb. shredded medium Cheddar cheese
1   can of crushed pineapple, drained
      toasted almonds
      small shrimp
      coconut

1. Stew chickens in enough water to cover them, adding onion, celery, peppercorns and chicken bouillon cubes.

2. Cook until done. Remove chicken reserving cooking liquid. Debone chicken, cut in bite-size pieces and set aside.

188

3. Make a white sauce with 2 cups of chicken liquid, butter and flour.

4. Add a dash of curry (optional); add sauce to chicken. Stir to coat chicken.

5. Have the selection of condiments in bowls on the table in this order: tomatoes, onion, Chinese noodles, celery, black and green olives, cheese, pineapple, almonds, shrimp and coconut.

6. Make a "mountain" of rice topped with chicken and condiments on each plate; top it off with a sprinkle of coconut (the "snow").

Ruby and Olive Mayo, circa 1945
Jim Parsons Jr. Collection

Drop Into Sandpoint
Foster Cline, MD.

Fish & Seafood

Keepers, circa 1900
Jim Parsons Jr. Collection

Baked White Fish with Spinach En Papillote
Serves one

1	sheet parchment paper, 12" x 18"
1	tsp. olive oil
1	cup baby spinach leaves, washed and dried
8	oz. sole or whitefish fillet, boned and skinned
	salt and pepper to taste

Relish

1	apple, peeled and grated
	juice and zest of ½ lime

Preheat oven 425°.

1. Fold parchment paper in half. Cut teardrop shape so when it opens it is a heart.

2. Lightly brush paper with oil. Mound spinach on one side of heart.

3. Season fish and place on top of spinach.

4. Fold other side of paper over and crimp edge all around. Make a continuous small fold to seal fish.

5. Place on cookie sheet and bake for about 11 minutes.

6. To make relish grate apple (don't use skin). Add zest and lime juice. Mix together.

7. Cut pouch open and garnish with relish.

Basil Shrimp with Feta and Orzo

Serves two

½	cup uncooked orzo
¾	lb. peeled and deveined shrimp
2	tsp. olive oil
1	cup diced tomatoes
¾	cup sliced green onions
3	medium cloves garlic, minced
½	cup feta cheese
½	tsp. grated lemon rind
1	tbsp. fresh lemon juice
¼	tsp. salt and black pepper
¼	cup fresh basil, chopped

Preheat oven to 450°.

1. Cook orzo in boiling water for 5 minutes; drain and place in large bowl. Stir in 1 teaspoon olive oil and next 7 ingredients. (Reserve other teaspoon of olive oil to drizzle over top.)

2. Place orzo mixture into large shallow baking pan.

3. Combine shrimp and basil and arrange shrimp on orzo mixture.

4. Bake for 25 minutes or until shrimp are done.

5. Drizzle remaining olive oil on top.

Bourbon Glazed Salmon

Serves eight

Marinade Ingredients

1	cup packed brown sugar
6	tbsp. bourbon
¼	cup low-sodium soy sauce
2	tbsp. fresh lime juice
2	tsp. fresh ginger, peeled and grated
½	tsp. salt
¼	tsp. freshly ground pepper
2	garlic cloves, crushed

Fish

8	6 oz. salmon fillets, about 1" thick
	cooking spray
4	tsp. toasted sesame seeds
½	cup thinly sliced green onions
	Marinating time 30 minutes.

1. Combine marinade ingredients in large zip-top plastic bag; add salmon fillets. Seal bag and marinate in refrigerator 30 minutes, turning bag once. Remove fillets from bag and discard marinade.

2. Preheat broiler or grill. Place fillets on broiler pan coated with cooking spray. Broil 11 minutes or until fish flakes easily when tested with fork.

3. Sprinkle each fillet with ½ teaspoon sesame seeds and 1 tablespoon green onions and serve.

Butterflied Trout in Lemon Caper Butter

4	butterflied whole trout
	salt and freshly ground black pepper
	flour for dredging
	olive oil for sautéing
2	tbsp. butter plus 1 tbsp.
2	lemons, supremed and cut into ½" pieces
1	tbsp. capers
	toasted croutons-recipe follows
¼	cup dry white wine
1	tsp. lemon juice
¼	cup parsley leaves, chopped

1. Lay out trout with skin down and flesh open like a book. With sharp knife cut out backbone. Keep head and tail attached. Season both sides with salt and pepper.

2. Dredge both sides of trout with flour. Shake off any excess. Heat large sauté pan on high. Use enough olive oil to lightly coat pan. Heat oil until it shimmers. Carefully add trout flesh side down. Start at tail and lay away from you towards head. May need to cook trout in batches. Cook until golden brown on both sides. Remove and keep warm on platter.

3. Once trout is cooked, return pan to medium high heat and remove all but 1 tablespoon of oil. Add 2 tablespoons butter and cook until it begins to brown and smell nutty, about 3 minutes.

4. Add capers, lemons, croutons, white wine, and lemon juice and cook. Stir for 2 minutes. Add remaining butter and remove from heat. Stir in parsley and pour over trout.

Toasted Croutons

3   tbsp. olive oil
4   ½" slices white bread, crust removed and cut into ¼" cubes
       salt and pepper to taste

1. Heat large sauté pan over high heat. Add olive oil and heat. When oil is hot add the bread cubes and cook. Stir until toasted and golden, about 10 minutes.

2. Season with salt and pepper. Remove from heat and cool.

Monk Shelman,Moyie River circa 1950s.
Jim Parsons Jr. Collection

California Jalapeño Trout
Serves eight

4	whole trout, cleaned
3	medium fresh jalapeño peppers, chopped
4	medium green onions, chopped
1	bunch cilantro, chopped
½	cup diced bell pepper
½	cup peeled, diced ripe mango
¼	cup extra virgin olive oil
2	tbsp. lime juice
	garlic salt to taste
	fresh ground black pepper to taste

Preheat grill to medium heat. Place rack 3" over coals.

1. In medium bowl, mix together jalapeño, green onions, cilantro, bell pepper, mango, olive oil garlic salt and black pepper. Set aside.

2. Lightly coat 4 squares foil with olive oil or cooking spray. Place fish diagonally on foil. Stuff each with ¼ mango stuffing. (If all of it does not fit inside fish place remainder on top of fish.) Fold remaining corners of foil over body of fish.

3. Cook packets on both side for about 20 minutes on each side. Fish will flake.

Recipe is easy on budget, waistline, and tastebuds. Recipe can be used on any kind of fish.

Crabmeat Casserole
Serves eight

2	tbsp. butter
1	14 oz. can artichoke hearts, coarsely chopped
1	lb. fresh crabmeat in chunks
½	lb. fresh mushrooms, chopped

Sauce

4	tbsp. butter
2½	tbsp. flour
1	cup fat free half and half
½	tsp. salt
1	tbsp. Worcestershire sauce
¼	cup medium dry sherry
½	tsp. paprika or to taste
	dash ground red pepper
¼	tsp. pepper to taste
⅓	cup grated Parmesan cheese
¼	cup parsley, chopped

Preheat oven to 375°.

1. Sauté mushrooms in 2 tablespoons butter. Place chopped artichokes in bottom of baking dish, sprinkle with crab meat and top with sautéed mushrooms.

2. For sauce melt remaining butter in saucepan; add rest of ingredients except cheese and parsley.

3. Cook, stirring well after each ingredient is added, to form smooth sauce. Pour sauce over artichoke and crab layers. Sprinkle cheese on top. Bake 20 minutes. Sprinkle with chopped parsley.

Deviled Clams
Serves six

1½	cups clams, chopped
2	tbsp. butter
½	small white onion, minced
1	tsp. Worcestershire sauce
1	tbsp. flour
½	cup milk
1	cup clam juice
1	cup bread crumbs about 4 slices
1	egg, beaten
	pinch cayenne pepper

Preheat oven to 350°.

1. Drain clams and save juice. Simmer onions in butter until golden.

2. Stir in flour, milk and clam juice; stir until smooth.

3. Add breadcrumbs, egg, and clams.

4. Cook stirring until it is thick.

5. Add salt, cayenne pepper and Worcestershire sauce.

6. Butter shells or ramekins and fill with clam mixture. Sprinkle with buttered bread crumbs.

7. Bake until light brown.

Dirty Shrimp
Serves two

5	tsp. butter
1	tsp. Worcestershire sauce
2	garlic cloves, minced
¼	tsp. cayenne pepper
½	tsp. freshly ground pepper
½	tsp. salt
½	tsp. thyme
1	tsp. basil
½	tsp. dried oregano
1	lb. medium shrimp shelled and deveined
4	cups beer

1. Melt butter in large skillet. Add Worcesterhire, garlic, red and black pepper, salt, thyme, basil and oregano.

2. Cook for about 1 minute. Add shrimp and cook 2 to 3 minutes. Stir to coat shrimp evenly.

3. Add beer, cover and cook until done, about 2 to 3 minutes.

4. Serve with French bread to dip in sauce or over rice.

Fish in Foil
Serves two

2   rainbow trout fillets
1   tbsp. olive oil
2   tsp. garlic salt
1   tsp. freshly ground pepper
1   fresh jalapeño pepper, sliced
1   fresh lemon, slice

Preheat oven to 400°.

1. Rinse fish and pat dry. Rub fillets with olive oil. Season with garlic salt and black pepper.

2. Place each fillet on a large sheet of aluminum foil. Top with jalapeño slices. Squeeze juice from end of lemons over fish. Arrange lemon slices on top of fillets.

3. Seal carefully the edges of foil. Place packets on baking sheet.

4. Bake for 15 to 20 minutes depending on size of fish. Fish is done when it flakes easily on a fork.

Getting It On "Cioppino"
Serves six to eight

2	tbsp. marjoram
1	tbsp. rosemary
1	tbsp. sage
1	tbsp. thyme
1	tbsp. basil
½	cup fresh parsley, chopped
4	garlic cloves, minced
4	small red chili peppers (dried), chopped
1	large bunch Swiss chard (or spinach), chopped
1-2	cups dry red or white wine
25-40	clams or mussels
2-3	crabs, cracked and cut up
1½-2	lbs. prawns or shrimp
2	lbs. white (firm) fish
2-3	cans solid pack tomatoes
6	oz. can tomato paste
¾	cup olive oil
2	tbsp. salt and pepper

If you use fresh herbs, double amount.

1. In large bowl toss all herbs together with chard and mix well by hand.

2. In large kettle, arrange clams or mussels in bottom and sprinkle layer of herb mixture over them.

3. Add crab and a layer of herbs followed by prawns and herbs and, finally, fish and herbs. Mix together one cup wine, tomatoes, tomato paste, oil, salt and pepper and pour over seafood in kettle.

4. Cook at moderate heat until it boils, then simmer about 30 to 40 minutes.

5. Add remaining wine 10 minutes before serving.

This is great with French bread, a green salad and more wine!

The Girl on the Beach, circa 1914
The Bonner County Historical Society Collection

Grilled Citrus Salmon
Serves six

3	lbs. fresh salmon fillets
1½	tbsp. lemon juice
2	tbsp. olive oil
1	tbsp. butter
1	tbsp. Dijon mustard
4	cloves garlic, minced
2	pinches cayenne pepper
2	pinches of salt
1	tsp. fresh basil
1	tsp. fresh dill
2	tsp. capers

Preheat oven to 350°.

1. Combine in small sauce pan lemon juice, olive oil, butter, mustard, garlic, pepper, salt, basil, dill and capers.

2. Bring to a boil while stirring. Reduce heat and simmer for 5 minutes.

3. Place fillets on heavy foil and cover them evenly with sauce.

4. Place on grill and cover. Cook 10 to 12 minutes over medium to hot coals.

5. You may wrap fish in foil and bake in oven for 15 to 20 minutes.

Halibut Onion Crunch

Serves six

4	halibut fillets or steaks
3	tbsp. cooking oil
1½	tsp. lemon juice
½	tsp. salt
	dash pepper
	dash dry mustard
¼	tsp. marjoram
¼	tsp. garlic salt
⅓	cup canned French fried onions, crumbled
3	tbsp. grated Parmesan cheese

Preheat oven to 450°.

1. Combine oil, lemon juice, salt, pepper, mustard, marjoram and garlic salt.

2. Pour mixture over fish and marinate 20 minutes; turn the fish once.

3. Transfer fish to buttered baking dish and sprinkle with French fried onions and cheese.

4. Bake for 20 minutes or until fish flakes with a fork.

Herbed Halibut
Serves six

3   lbs. halibut fillet, or 6 halibut steaks

Marinade

4   tbsp. melted butter
2   garlic cloves, minced
½   tsp. salt
     dash freshly ground pepper
2   tbsp. fresh lemon juice
½   cup dry white wine
1   tsp. fresh dill or fresh tarragon
2   tbsp. fresh parsley, chopped
     parsley sprigs
     lemon wedges

1. Combine the first 8 ingredients for the marinade.

2. Arrange fish in one layer in shallow pan. Pour marinade over the fish. Cover and marinate about 1 hour.

3. Remove fish from marinade and broil or grill. Fish should be 2 to 4" from heat source; cook about 5 minutes per side. Baste with marinade. Cook until fish flakes with fork.

4. Garnish with parsley and lemon wedges and serve.

Keepers
Grilled trout or salmon

1½   lbs. salmon or trout with skin left on
¼   cup olive oil
1   tbsp. fresh thyme, chopped or 1 tsp. dry thyme
¼   tsp. hot red pepper flakes
1   tbsp. lemon juice
3   tbsp. butter
    salt and pepper to taste
    fresh parsley, chopped

1. Pour oil into flat dish and add fish. Turn fish to coat all sides.

2. Sprinkle with salt, pepper, thyme, hot pepper flakes and lemon juice.

3. Cover with plastic wrap and let stand at room temperature for about 10 to 15 minutes.

4. Remove fish from marinade. Place fillets skin side down on medium heated grill.

5. Turn after 2 or 3 minutes. Cooking time depends on thickness of fillets and temperature of grill.

6. For sauce pour marinade into sauce pan and add 3 tablespoons butter and bring to boil.

7. Pour over fish and sprinkle with fresh chopped parsley.

Monk Shelman's Catch, Moyie River circa 1950s
Jim Parsons Jr. Collection

Lime Halibut Kabobs

Serves four

1	lb. halibut, skinned
¼	cup fresh lime juice
¼	cup dry white wine
1	tbsp. olive or cooking oil
1	small clove garlic, pressed or minced
½	tsp. crushed dried basil
¼	tsp.crushed dried oregano
	salt to taste
	freshly ground pepper to taste
1	medium zucchini
1	medium yellow squash
1	medium red bell pepper

1. Cut halibut into 1" cubes.

2. Cut squash into ½" slices. Cut red pepper into 1" pieces.

3. In medium bowl, stir together lime juice, wine, oil, garlic, basil, oregano, salt and pepper. Add fish and stir until coated. Cover and marinate at room temperature for 30 minutes, stirring gently several times.

4. Microwave squash and pepper with 1 tablespoon water for 2 minutes. Drain and let stand until cool.

3. On 4 wooden skewers, alternately thread fish cubes, squash and red pepper. Place in microwave-safe baking dish. Pour reserved marinade over kabobs.

4. Cover and cook in microwave on high, just until fish flakes with fork (3 to 4 minutes). Rearrange skewers halfway through cooking time so fish will cook evenly.

Can be cooked on grill for few minutes on each side; turn and brush with reserved marinade.

Peppery Garlic Shrimp with Sherry Sauce
Serves two

You will need two serving portions of linguini pasta.

Sauce

½	cup cream sherry
5½	tbsp. olive oil
2	tbsp. fresh lemon juice
7	garlic cloves, minced
4	drops of Tabasco sauce
3	tbsp. chopped fresh parsley
12	ounces of large shrimp uncooked, peeled and deveined

1. For sauce pour sherry, 1 tablespoon oil, lemon juice, garlic and Tabasco into small heavy sauce pan and bring to boil. Boil until reduced to ¼ cup (about 7 minutes).

2. Transfer mixture to blender. With machine running, gradually add 3 tablespoons oil. Blend until smooth. Season with salt and pepper. Add parsley and blend, pulsing, using on and off turns.

3. Cook pasta according to package directions. Drain and add ½ tablespoon oil to cooked pasta. Keep warm.

4. To cook the shrimp, heat remaining tablespoon oil and 1 thinly sliced garlic clove over high heat. Add shrimp and sauté about 2-3 minutes.

5. Toss sauce with cooked pasta and arrange shrimp on top of pasta. Sprinkle with chopped parsley and serve.

This is a quick and tasty dish. Sauce can be made several hours in advance.

Salmon and Leek Pie
Serve six

Pie

4	large leeks
2	tbsp. unsalted butter
2¼	lbs. salmon fillet, skinned and boned
¼	cup fresh dill, chopped
1	tsp. lime zest
1½	tsp. coarse salt
¼	tsp. black pepper, freshly ground
1	large egg
1	tbsp. water
1	17¼ oz. package frozen puff pastry sheets, thawed

Sauce

plain yogurt
pinch of sugar
2-3 fresh dill sprigs, chopped

Preheat oven to 350°.

1. To prepare leeks cut white and pale green parts of leeks crosswise into ½" thick slices. Wash leeks well in bowl of cold water. Drain, and pat dry.

2. In large skillet cook leeks in butter over moderate heat, stirring until tender, about 12 minutes. Cool.

3. To prepare pie, cut salmon into roughly ¾" pieces and in a bowl toss with leeks, dill, zest, salt and pepper until well combined.

4. In small bowl whisk egg and water to make an egg wash.

5. For pastry lightly flour rolling surface and rolling pin. Roll 1 puff pastry sheet into a 10" square and other into a 12" square.

6. Transfer the 10" pastry square to floured large baking sheet and mound salmon filling in center, forming round 8" in diameter. Brush edges of pastry evenly with some egg wash.

7. Carefully drape remaining pastry square over salmon and gently press edges together to seal. With sharp knife trim edges of pastry to form 10" round. Crimp edges and cut 4 steam vents on top of crust.

8. Brush evenly with some remaining egg wash. Chill pie, loosely covered, at least 1 hour and up to 3 hours.

9. Bake at 350° for 30 minutes or until pastry is brown.

Garnish with fresh dill and serve.

Scallops with Tomato and Garlic
Serves four

1½	lbs. sea scallops
1	lb. fresh linguini pasta
¼	cup milk
½	cup flour
2	tbsp. olive oil
4	cups canned imported Italian tomatoes, drained and chopped
4	tbsp. chopped fresh basil
6	tbsp. corn oil
4	tbsp. butter
2	tbsp. finely chopped garlic
2	tbsp. finely chopped parsley

1. Put scallops in mixing bowl; add milk, salt and pepper. In a large pot, boil water for pasta.

2. Cook pasta as directed, and drain.

3. Heat olive oil in heavy skillet; add tomatoes, salt and pepper. Bring to boil and let cook for 5 minutes. Add basil and remove from heat. Heat corn oil in skillet large enough to hold scallops in one layer. Put flour in flat dish.

4. Drain scallops but do not pat dry. Dredge scallops in flour and shake off excess. Put scallops in hot oil and cook for about 5 minutes or until brown on one side. Turn and cook about 5 minutes on the other side.

5. To assemble, heat tomato sauce and spoon over pasta. When scallops are cooked, transfer them to pasta and tomato sauce.

6. Pour off fat from skillet in which scallops were cooked. Wipe out skillet. Add butter and cook, swirling it around until it starts to brown and takes on hazelnut color. Add garlic and pour this mixture over scallops

Sprinkle with parsley and serve.

Scallops with Hazelnuts and Pears

Serves three to four

20   oz. scallops
½   cup skinned hazelnuts
¾   cup seedless grapes
1   large pear, peeled, cut into ¾" cubes
¾   cup dry white wine
2   tbsp. unsalted butter
½   lemon, juiced
      nutmeg to garnish

1. Sauté hazelnuts in 1 tablespoon butter until light golden brown. Remove from pan. Sauté grapes and pear cubes for about 3 minutes. Add ½ cup wine and continue cooking until pear cubes are soft. Pour lemon juice on fruit and remove from pan. Save juices.

2. Increase heat, and lightly brown scallops. Add ¼ cup of same wine used above along with nuts, juices, fruit and 1 tablespoon butter to pan and cook scallops until they are done. Don't over cook!

3. Place scallops in small individual gratin dishes. Pour juices over them and lightly sprinkle with nutmeg and serve.

Basmati rice is a good accompaniment.

Seafood Lasagna
Serves ten

½	cup margarine or butter
2	cloves garlic, crushed
½	cup flour
½	tsp. salt
2	cups milk
2	cups chicken broth
2	cups Mozzarella cheese
½	cup green onions, sliced
1	tsp. dried basil leaves
¼	tsp. pepper
8	oz. uncooked lasagna noodles
1	cup cottage cheese
1	7½ oz. can drained crab meat or fresh crab
1½	4½ oz. can tiny shrimp or fresh shrimp
½	cup Parmesan cheese

Preheat oven to 350°.

1. Melt butter and add garlic. Stir in flour and salt. Stir until bubbly. Whisk in milk and broth. Heat to boil, stirring constantly for one minute. Simmer and whisk over medium heat until sauce is thick, about 5 to 10 min. Add green onions, salt, pepper and basil. Set Aside.

2. In a 9" x 13" pan layer 1½ cup sauce, 4 uncooked noodles, cottage cheese, and seafood. Repeat with remaining sauce, noodles and mozzarella cheese. Sprinkle Parmesan cheese on top. Bake uncovered for 35 to 40 minutes. Let stand 15 minutes.

Seafood Soufflé

Serves six to eight

6	slices of day old bread
1	cup half and half
6	hard-boiled eggs sliced and chopped
1	cup mayonnaise
1	tbsp. grated onion
3	drops of Tabasco
	salt and pepper to taste
½	lb. crab
½	lb. shrimp
1	cup buttered bread crumbs

1. Prepare by pouring the half and half over bread cubes. Chop eggs and add mayonnaise, onion, Tabasco, salt and pepper. Mix gently. Mix in seafood. Butter 8" x 8" baking dish and place mixture in dish. Cover with foil and refrigerate overnight.

2. Two hours before serving remove foil and add bread crumbs. Bake at 350° for 30 minutes.

This is an excellent main dish for brunch or lunch; serve with fresh fruit.

Sea Scallops with Peppercorn Sauce

Serves four

16	sea scallops
2	tbsp. butter
¼	cup dry white wine
¼	cup brandy
2	tbsp. minced shallots
4	garlic cloves, minced
1	cup whipping cream
3	tbsp. sour cream
2	tsp. cracked black pepper

1. To prepare scallops melt butter in pan, sear dry scallops in very hot pan 1 or 2 minutes and turn to repeat on other side. Scallops should be brown, but not overcooked. Remove from pan and keep warm.

2. Add wine, brandy, shallots and garlic to skillet and boil, scraping up browned bits. Boil 1 minute; add cream. Boil until reduced, about 5 minutes. Remove from heat; add sour cream and cracked pepper.

Serve with rice, pasta or mashed potatoes. Garnish with fresh chopped chives.

The sauce is also good with New York Steaks. Double cracked pepper to 4 tablespoons. To cut back fat in this recipe, use ½ cup cream and ½ cup clam broth or fish stock.

223

Shrimp Curry Un Momento

Serves four

1   lb. large shrimp, peeled
1   tsp. olive oil

Sauce

½   cup orange marmalade
¾   cup mild salsa
1   large tomato, diced
1   tsp. curry powder

1. Sauté shrimp in olive oil. Drain off excess liquid. Mix ingredients for sauce and add to shrimp. Warm through.

2. Spoon over rice or angel hair pasta. Complete the meal with large green or spinach salad.

Shrimp Stroganoff
Serves four to six

6	tbsp. butter
1½-2	lbs. shrimp, shelled and cleaned
1½	lbs. fresh mushrooms, sliced
3	tbsp. minced onion
1	clove garlic, minced
3	tbsp. flour
1	cup chicken stock or broth (or part white wine)
1	tsp. catsup
1	tsp. Worcestershire sauce
½	pint sour cream
1	tbsp. fresh dill or parsley, chopped

1. Melt half of the butter in large skillet. Add shrimp and cook, turning several times, for 3-5 minutes or until pink. Remove shrimp from the pan and keep warm.

2. In the same pan, melt remaining butter; add mushrooms and sauté for 2 minutes. Add onion and garlic, sauté until tender but not browned, about 5 minutes (add a little more butter if necessary).

3. Stir in flour, gradually add stock or broth. Cook, stirring until thickened. Add catsup and Worcestershire. Remove from heat. Blend in sour cream, dill and shrimp.

4. Spoon over rice and serve.

Spicy Halibut with Citrus Salsa

Serves four

Salsa

4   medium navel oranges, peeled and sectioned
½   cup chopped red onion
¼   cup fresh lime juice
¼   cup minced fresh cilantro or parsley
¼   tsp. crushed red pepper flakes
1   pressed garlic clove
1   tsp. grated orange peel

Fish

1   lb. halibut or cod fillets
½   tsp. salt
2   tsp. ground coriander, or to taste
1¼   tsp. pepper, or to taste
2   tsp. ground cumin

1. To prepare salsa combine the first 7 ingredients plus ¼ teaspoon salt and ¼ teaspoon pepper. Cover and chill.

2. Prepare grill. Combine coriander, cumin and remaining salt and pepper; rub over both sides of fillets.

3. Grill, covered, over medium high heat or broil 4 to 6 inches from heat until fish flakes easily with a fork (four to six minutes per side).

4. Serve fish with citrus salsa.

226

Taku Grilled Salmon
Serves eight

⅓	cup butter
⅔	cup brown sugar
2	tbsp. lemon juice
1	tbsp. dry white wine
8	10-12 oz. salmon fillets

1. In medium sauce pan melt butter over medium heat. Stir in brown sugar until dissolved.

2. Add lemon juice and wine. Stir and heat through, about 5 minutes.

3. Place fillets in a well-greased grill basket.

4. Grill on an uncovered grill directly over medium coals for 4-6 minutes per ½" thickness or until fish flakes when tested with fork. Turn once during cooking; brush occasionally with basting sauce.

"Over the Back Fence." Violet Leahy with bucket. She taught at The Elmira School in 1910.

Robert Gunter Collection

Vegetables, Pasta,
Potatoes & Rice

Autum Comes to Schweitzer
Foster Cline, MD.

Vegetables, Potatoes, Pasta & Rice

"Celebrating the Harvest," Trestle Creek, Mr. & Mrs. Don Eaton. circa, 1900. The Bonner County Historical Society Collection

Allene's Pilaf

Serves four

¼	cup butter or margarine
1	small onion, chopped
¼	cup slivered almonds
¼	cup raisins
1	cup rice
2	cups hot chicken broth

Preheat oven to 375°.

1. Grease a 1½ quart casserole.

2. In saucepan melt butter and sauté chopped onion, almonds and raisins until golden brown.

3. Add rice, hot chicken broth and mix well.

4. Place in covered casserole and bake for 30 minutes or until all of liquid is absorbed.

Allene's Rice is an excellent accompaniment with meat, fish or as a main vegetarian dish.

Asparagus Tarragon Custard with Red Bell Pepper sauce

Serves four

Custard

1	lb. asparagus, trimmed
¼	cup whipping cream
¼	cup half and half
3	egg yolks
¼	tsp. dried tarragon
¼	tsp. salt
¼	tsp. pepper
1	tbsp. butter

Sauce

¼	cup olive oil
1¼	lbs. red bell peppers, coarsely chopped
1	tsp. dried tarragon
1	bay leaf
½	tsp. salt
½	cup chicken stock
	additional salt to taste
	pepper to taste

Position rack in center of oven and preheat to 325°.

1. To prepare custard, butter four 6 oz. custard cups. Cook asparagus in large pot of boiling salted water until tender, about 5 minutes. Drain.

2. Transfer to bowl of ice water and cool. Drain and pat dry. Cut off tips and reserve for garnish. Cut asparagus stalks into ½" pieces.

3. Pureé asparagus stalks in processor. Transfer pureé to bowl. Whisk in cream, half and half, egg yolks, tarragon, salt and pepper.

4. Ladle mixture into prepared custard cups. Arrange cups in heavy large baking pan at least 2" high. Add enough hot water to pan to come halfway up sides of cups.

5. Bake until custards are set, about 1 hour. Remove custards from water and cool 5 minutes.

6. Melt butter in heavy medium skillet, add asparagus tips, season with salt and pepper. Set aside.

7. To remove custards from cups run a small sharp knife around custard to loosen. Invert each cup on individual serving plates.

Sauce

1. Heat oil in heavy large saucepan over low heat. Add peppers, tarragon, bay leaf and salt. Cook until peppers are very tender (about 30 minutes). Cool slightly; discard bay leaf. Transfer peppers to processor and pureé until smooth. Strain pureé through sieve. Season with salt and pepper. Thin sauce with chicken stock to desired consistency. Sauce can be prepared a day ahead.

2. Heat red bell pepper sauce to simmer and spoon sauce around custards. Sprinkle asparagus tips over sauce and serve.

Baked Hungarian Noodles
Serves six to eight

½	lb. fine noodles
2	cups cream style cottage cheese
2	cups sour cream
½	cup onion, minced
3	cloves garlic, minced
2	tbsp. Worcestershire sauce
2	dashes Tabasco sauce
2	tbsp. poppy seeds
1	tsp. salt
	freshly ground pepper to taste

Garnish

paprika
Parmesan cheese
parsley

Preheat oven to 350°.

1. Cook noodles in boiling, salted water until tender. Drain. Combine cooked noodles with next nine ingredients.

2. Place in buttered casserole. Bake for 30 minutes or until hot. Sprinkle with paprika, Parmesan cheese, and parsley.

234

Baked Potato Topping without Butter
Serves four

2	cups sliced fresh mushrooms
1	medium onion, chopped
⅓	cup shredded carrots
¾	cup chicken broth
1	tbsp. cornstarch
1	tbsp. Dijon mustard
¼	tsp. pepper or to taste
	Parmesan cheese

1. Combine the mushrooms, onion, carrots and chicken broth in a 1½ quart microwave safe casserole.

2. Microwave covered on high for 5 to 7 minutes or until vegetables are cooked.

3. In a small bowl stir together cornstarch, mustard and pepper. Stir in vegetables. Cook on high 2 to 3 minutes stirring every minute until sauce is thickened and bubbly, about 3 minutes.

4. Split open baked potatoes. Mash center slightly with fork. Season to taste with salt and pepper. Pour sauce on top. If desired, sprinkle with Parmesan cheese.

Cajun Rice
Serves eight

2	cups rice, uncooked
2½	cups water
2	tbsp. melted butter
1	14 oz. can chicken broth
2	tbsp. finely chopped onion
2	tbsp. finely chopped celery
2	tbsp. minced garlic cloves
½	tsp. salt
	pinch cayenne and freshly ground pepper
1	tsp. paprika

1. In large saucepan, bring water and butter to a boil. Add all other ingredients and cook for 20 to 30 minutes or until the rice is done.

2. Can also bake in 350° oven for about one hour.

Calico Bean Bake

Serves four to six

1	lb. hamburger
½	onion, chopped
½	lb. bacon, chopped (optional)
1½	cups catsup
1½	cups brown sugar
1	tbsp. dry mustard
1	tbsp. salt
2-3	tsp. vinegar
1	lb. can kidney beans, drained
1	lb. can pork and beans
1	lb. can baby lima beans or butter beans (Can use garbanzo or any type of bean/lentils)

1. Brown hamburger, onions and bacon in skillet.

2. Add catsup, brown sugar, dry mustard, salt, vinegar, kidney beans, pork and beans and lima beans.

3. Put everything together into a crock pot and cook on high for 2 to 4 hours and then to low heat. The longer this simmers the better. It freezes well.

Train Station, circa 1950s
Jim Parsons Jr. Collection

Cheese and Chile Rice

Serves eight to ten

2	cups water
1	tbsp. butter
½	tsp. salt
2	cups long grain instant rice
½	lb. (2 cups) Monterey Jack cheese, shredded
1	4 oz. can diced green chilies
1	cup sour cream
3	tbsp. butter
¼	cup Cheddar cheese, grated
	garnish rice with paprika

Preheat oven to 350°.

1. Cook rice with water, butter and salt.

2. Mix next 5 ingredients together, add cooked rice and pour into and 8" x 8" pan.

3. Sprinkle with paprika and bake for 30 minutes.

Chile Relleno Casserole

Serves six to eight

2	4 oz. cans whole green chilies
1	lb. Monterey Jack cheese, shredded
½	cup cottage cheese
1	16 oz. can/jar salsa

Batter

3	eggs
2½	cups milk (substitute with ½ cream)
1	cup Bisquick
1	tsp. salt

Preheat oven to 350°.

1. Layer one can of chilies that are cut to lie flat in 9" x 13" pan. Follow with ½ of shredded cheese and cottage cheese.

2. For batter, beat eggs, milk, Bisquick and salt. Mix well. The batter will be thin.

3. Pour batter over casserole and layer on second can of chilies and jack cheese.

4. Bake 40 minutes. Serve with salsa of your choice.

Eggplant and Tomato Gratin

Serves six to eight

¼	cup olive oil
1	cup chopped onion
2	large eggplant, peeled and cubed
1	cup water
2-3	garlic cloves, chopped
1	14.5 oz. can diced tomatoes
1	8 oz. can tomato sauce
½	tsp. basil
½	cup fine dry bread crumbs (can use crushed saltines)
1	cup Cheddar cheese, grated

Preheat oven to 375°.

1. In large fry pan, add oil and onion. Sauté onion for a few minutes. Add cubed eggplant and coat as much as possible with the oil. Add water and cook until eggplant is soft adding garlic just toward the end of this process.

2. In a 2 quart casserole, place cooked eggplant, tomatoes, tomato sauce, basil, bread crumbs and ½ cup cheese. Mix together and sprinkle remaining cheese on top. Bake covered for 30 minutes or microwave for 8 minutes.

3. Serve with green salad and crusty sourdough bread.

Greek Style Spinach Turnovers
Serves six

1	pkg. frozen patty shells thawed
½	cup chopped onion
1	tbsp. oil
1	10 oz. pkg. frozen spinach, thawed, chopped and drained
1	cup crumbled feta cheese
1	cup cottage cheese
1	egg, beaten
¾	tsp. salt
¾	tsp. pepper

Preheat oven to 400°.

1. Roll out each patty shell between sheets of waxed paper to form 7½" circle and chill.

2. In saucepan, sauté onion in oil until tender. Add spinach; cook and stir until all liquid evaporates. Set aside and cool.

3. Stir in cheeses, egg, salt and pepper.

4. Take out one chilled shell at a time and remove waxed paper. If pastry sticks, place in freezer for a few minutes.

5. Place ½ cup spinach mixture in center of pastry. Fold over to form semicircle. Fold edges over and press well to seal.

6. Carefully transfer to ungreased cookie sheet and bake for 30 to 35 minutes or until pastry is golden brown.

Green Chile Pie
Serves six

12   oz. Monterey Jack cheese
4   oz. mozzarella cheese
1   medium onion, peeled and quartered
1   4 oz. can mild or hot green chopped chilies
1   tbsp. butter
1   tbsp. corn oil
3   poblano chile peppers, roasted and peeled
3   tomatoes cored and quartered or a 10 oz. can, diced
⅓   cup cream
      peanut oil as needed
6   corn tortillas
8   oz. cream cheese, softened
      salt to taste

Garnish

3   corn tortillas quartered and fried crisp
1   tomato, chopped
1   head lettuce, thinly sliced
6   sprigs fresh cilantro or parsley,
      black olives

Preheat oven to 350°.

1. Shred cheeses and set aside.

2. In 12" skillet, sauté the onion and chopped green chiles in butter and oil until onion is soft.

3. Stem and seed fresh roasted poblano chilies, cut into narrow strips. Add to skillet and continue

244

cooking for about 1 minute.

4. Dice fresh tomatoes; discard large pieces of skin. Gently stir into the skillet. Remove from heat and stir in the cream. Salt to taste.

5. For tortillas heat about 1" of peanut oil in skillet that is large enough to hold tortilla. Immerse tortillas one at a time. Cook only long enough to soften tortilla. Remove from skillet and press between layers of paper towel to remove excess oil.

6. Assemble casserole in buttered 10" to 12" pie tin. Spread each tortilla with about 1/6 of the cream cheese. Place a tortilla in pan and spread with some of the vegetable mixture. Add some shredded cheese.

7. Repeat this for six layers. Spoon any remaining vegetable mixture around stack and cover with the remaining cheese.

8. Bake for 20 to 25 minutes until the cheese is melted and stack is lightly browned.

9. Let stand for at least 5 minutes. Cut into wedges, garnish and serve.

Grilled Portabellas with Couscous
Serves 4

4	portabella mushroom caps about 4" to 5" in diameter
2	tbsp. olive oil
2	tsp. lemon juice
4	tsp. balsamic vinegar
¼	tsp fresh ground black pepper
¾	cup vegetable or chicken broth
½	cup whole-wheat couscous or regular couscous
2	tbsp. parsley, minced

Garnish with diced fresh vegetables: zucchini, red or green pepper, or green onions. Add to couscous

Preheat oven to 350°.

1. Prepare mushrooms by removing stems and gently wiping them clean.

2. Combine olive oil and lemon juice. Brush over smooth sides of mushrooms.

3. Grill mushrooms, smooth side down over high heat without turning until they are limp and begin to release their juices. About 3 to 5 minutes.

4. Transfer mushrooms to a 9" x 13" pan. Drizzle the vinegar over mushrooms. Add pepper and ¼ cup of the broth to pan.

5. Cover and bake until hot (about 5 to 10 minutes).

6. To make couscous bring the remaining ½ cup of broth to a boil and stir in couscous. Cover and remove from heat. Let stand until the liquid is absorbed, about 5 minutes.

7. Fluff couscous with a fork and stir in the parsley.

8. Set mushrooms smooth side down on a plate and top with couscous.

Honey Glazed Carrots
Serves eight

1½	quarts water
5	cups carrots
3	tbsp. chopped fresh parsley
2	tbsp. honey
½	tsp. salt
½	tsp. freshly grated orange peel
¼	tsp. fresh ground pepper

1. Bring water to a boil, add carrots and cook until tender. Drain well

2. Toss carrots in a large serving bowl with next 5 ingredients.

3. Prepare ahead of time and reheat in microwave.

Light and Cheesy Broccoli Casserole
Serves six to eight

1	10 oz. pkg. frozen chopped broccoli, thawed and drained
1	cup sour cream (Can use light cream or IMO.)
1	cup cottage cheese
½	cup Bisquick
½	cup margarine, melted
2	eggs
1	tomato, peeled and thinly sliced
¼	cup Parmesan cheese, grated

Preheat oven to 350°.

1. Grease lightly an 8"x8" baking dish. Spread chopped broccoli in bottom.

2. Beat sour cream, cottage cheese, Bisquick, margarine and eggs with a hand mixer for 1 minute.

3. Pour mixture over broccoli.

4. Arrange tomato slices on top; sprinkle with Parmesan cheese.

5. Bake for about 20 minutes or until golden brown. Insert knife in the center; when knife comes out clean casserole is done.

6. Cool 5 minutes before serving.

Linguini with White Clam Sauce

Serves six

2   6½ oz. cans clams, chopped or minced
1   bottle clam juice
¼   cup olive oil
3   cloves garlic, pressed
1   tbsp. cornstarch
2   tbsp. chopped parsley
1   lb. linguini
       Parmesan cheese, freshly grated

1. Drain clams and reserve liquid. Add bottled clam juice to make 1½ cups.

2. In saucepan, cook garlic in olive oil over medium heat until soft.

3. Dissolve cornstarch in clam liquid and add to saucepan with parsley.

4. Slowly bring to boil, reduce heat and simmer uncovered for 5 minutes. Add clams; simmer 2 to 3 minutes more.

5. Cook pasta.

6. Mix cooked pasta with clam sauce. Top with cheese if desired.

Marinated Tomatoes
Serves eight

Marinade

6   large red tomatoes, sliced
1   garlic clove, minced
½   tsp. dried or 2 tbsp. fresh thyme
¼   cup minced parsley
¼   cup thinly sliced green onions
1   tsp. salt
¼   tsp. pepper, freshly ground
¼   cup red or white vinegar
⅓   cup olive oil

Pour marinade over tomatoes and marinate for at least 2 hours.

Microwave Acorn Squash

Serves four

1   acorn squash

Filling

apple butter
orange marmalade
brown sugar and red wine

1. Cut squash in half and remove seeds.

2. Place squash cut side down in shallow glass pan with about ¼" of water. Do not crowd squash.

3. Cover and cook in the microwave for 6 to 7 minutes on high heat. Test with fork or toothpick.

4. Turn squash over and brush cavity and edges of squash with butter and add any of the following fillings: apple butter, orange marmalade, or tightly packed brown sugar with a few tablespoons of red wine.

5. Cover and return to microwave and cook for about 2 minutes or until filling is hot and melted.

Haugness Children, Circa 1910. (L to) Rachel Stueckle,
Haakon Haugness & Altona Wigen. See parents, 281.
Dagmar and Marvin Kirking Collection

Muffuletta Sandwich
Serves six

1	large round loaf of Italian or French bread 8" to 9"
1	cup brine-cured green olives, pitted and finely chopped
1	cup brine-cured black olives, pitted and finely chopped
½	cup extra-virgin olive oil
⅓	cup finely chopped fresh parsley
2	tsp. minced fresh oregano
1	garlic clove, minced
1	red bell pepper roasted, peeled, seeded and finely chopped
½	lemon, juiced
2	cups shredded lettuce
4	oz. mortadella or a soft salami, sliced
4	oz. soppressata or a hard salami, thinly sliced
1	cup chopped fresh tomatoes
2	cups shredded lettuce
4	oz. provolone, fontina or fresh mozzarella, thinly sliced

1. In small bowl combine olives, olive oil, parsley, oregano, garlic, red bell pepper and lemon juice.

2. Cover and refrigerate for at least 8 hours.

3. Split bread in half horizontally.

4. Remove most of soft inner bread to create a cavity in each half.

5. Drain olive mixture and save liquid.

254

6. Brush inside of each half of the bread generously with marinade.

7. Spread half of olive mixture in bottom half of loaf. Add layers of lettuce, mortadella, soppressata, provolone and tomatoes.

8. Top with remaining olive mixture and put on top half of the loaf.

9. Wrap sandwich tightly in plastic wrap and place on a large plate. Cover sandwich with another plate and weight it down with several pounds of canned goods.

10. Refrigerate for at least 30 minutes or up to 6 hours.

11. Unwrap and cut into wedges.

This is a wonderful sandwich to take on a boat, a picnic or for house guests. The longer it sits the better it gets. Put on extra lettuce when served.

Mushroom Supreme

1-2   lb. whole mushrooms
2   tbsp. butter
2   beef bouillon cubes
½   cup hot water
4   tbsp. butter
2   tbsp. flour
½   cup cream
       pinch of salt and pepper
½   cup bread crumbs
½   cup Parmesan cheese

Preheat oven to 350°.

1. Sauté mushrooms in 2 tablespoons butter and dissolve beef bouillon in hot water.

2. In a saucepan melt 4 tablespoons butter and blend with flour. Add cream, salt, pepper and blend in mushrooms and beef broth.

3. Pour mixture into buttered casserole dish; top with Parmesan cheese and bread crumbs.

4. Bake for 30 minutes.

Pickled Mushrooms
Makes one quart

1	cup red vinegar
2	whole cloves
½	cup cold water
5	whole peppercorns
½	bay leaf
2	tsp. salt
2	garlic cloves, peeled and crushed
1	lb. fresh mushrooms
1	tbsp. vegetable oil

1. In stainless steel or enamel 2 quart pan, combine first 7 ingredients and bring to boil over high heat.

2. Drop in mushrooms and reduce heat to low. Simmer uncovered for 10 minutes stirring occasionally.

3. Cool to room temperature.

4. To store, remove garlic and pour into a 1 quart jar. Slowly pour oil on top. Cover the jar with plastic wrap and cover tightly with jar lid.

5. Marinate for 2 days. The mushrooms will stay tasty in the refrigerator for a long time.

Grandmother Kristine Haugness showing her grandson, Matt Kirking, how to peel potatoes. See wedding picture, 281.

Portofino Pasta
Serves four

½	lb. angel hair pasta, cooked, drained and drizzled with olive oil
1	tbsp. olive oil
2	garlic cloves, chopped
8	oz. fresh mushrooms, sliced
1-2	scallions, chopped
4-5	oz. fresh spinach
½	cup parsley, chopped
2	fresh tomatoes, chopped
10-12	black olives, cut in half
	salt to taste

1. Sauté garlic in olive oil briefly. Add mushrooms and scallions; then add spinach, parsley, tomatoes and black olives.

2. Cook 5 to 8 minutes. Pour over cooked angel hair pasta.

3. Sprinkle with Parmesan cheese.

May add shrimp and clams to sauce. For more sauce, add chicken broth. Basil lovers can add fresh chopped basil along with Parmesan cheese.

Potatoes Dauphinaise
Serves eight to ten

6	potatoes, peeled and thinly sliced
	salt and pepper to taste
1	clove garlic
2	tbsp. butter
1	cup grated Gruyere cheese
2	eggs
2	cups heavy cream
¼	tsp. nutmeg

Preheat oven to 350°.

1. Season potatoes with salt and pepper. Place a layer of potoatoes in 2 quart baking dish rubbed with garlic and greased with butter.

2. Add layer of Gruyere and repeat. Alternate layers.

3. Beat eggs with cream and nutmeg. Pour over potatoes and cheese.

4. Bake 1 hour.

Rice d'Orange
Serves four to six

3   cups rice cooked in 4½ cups chicken broth
1   tbsp. butter
1   tsp. salt
½   tsp. thyme
½   cup chopped green onions
¼   cup raisins
¼   cup fresh orange juice
¼   cup sherry
½   tbsp. orange peel
½   cup Mandarin oranges

1. Melt butter and add salt, thyme, green onions, raisins, orange juice and sherry.

2. Cover and cook over low heat for about 5 minutes until raisins are plump.

3. Stir in rice and orange peel. Place in serving bowl and garnish with mandarin oranges.

This is a special accompaniment to pork tenderloin.

261

Rosemary Glazed Vidalia Onions

Serves four

1	cup dry red wine
2	tbsp. sugar
1	tbsp. fresh rosemary or 1 tsp. dried rosemary
1	tbsp. fresh lemon juice
	dash ground cloves
	freshly ground black pepper to taste
2	medium Vidalia or other sweet onions, unpeeled
	cooking spray
2	tbsp. olive oil

Preheat oven to 400°.

1. Combine first 6 ingredients in a small sauce pan; bring to a boil. Reduce heat to medium; cook uncovered until sauce is reduced to ½ cup. Set aside.

2. Cut onions lengthwise in half. Place onions, cut sides down in a small baking dish coated with cooking spray. Drizzle olive oil over onions.

3. Cover onions and bake for 25 minutes.

4. Uncover and bake for 20 minutes.

5. Turn onions over and pour wine mixture over onions. Bake for an additional 20 minutes or until onions are tender. Baste every 5 minutes.

6. Serve onions with wine mixture from the pan.

Royal Rice
Serves six to eight

1	12 oz. jar marinated artichoke hearts
1	cup rice
2	cups chicken broth
¼	tsp. salt
	pinch thyme
4	scallions, chopped
½	green pepper, diced
⅓	cup mayonnaise
¾	tsp. curry powder

1. Drain artichokes and reserve liquid.

2. In a covered saucepan cook rice in chicken broth.

3. When rice is done, add salt, thyme, scallions, artichokes and green pepper. Mix well.

4. Combine liquid from artichokes with the mayonnaise and curry. Gently toss rice mixture.

5. Serve warm as side a dish or chill and serve as luncheon salad.

Spanish Frittata
Serves eight

½   lb. cheese-onion or cheese-jalapeño bread, cut into ½" cubes
9   large eggs
2   cups milk
1   cup (4 oz.) shredded jack cheese
1   cup (4 oz.) shredded Cheddar cheese
1   can (7 oz.) diced green chilies
½   cup chopped onion
¼   cup chopped fresh cilantro
⅓   cup chopped fresh Anaheim chilies
2   tbsp. chopped parsley
1   tbsp. salt

Garnish

avocado slices
salsa, mild
sour cream

1. Spread bread evenly in a buttered 9" x 13" pan.

2. In a bowl, beat eggs and milk just to blend. Add jack cheese, Cheddar cheese, diced chilies, onion, fresh chopped cilantro, fresh chilies, parsley and salt. Pour evenly over bread.

3. Cover and chill at least 8 hours or overnight.

4. Uncover and bake 350° about 45 minutes or until the center barely jiggles when gently shaken, and top is lightly browned.

5. Cut into pieces and serve with mild salsa, sour cream and avocado slices.

Sweet Potato Casserole
Serves six to seven

6–7   sweet potatoes or 2 cans sweet potatoes, drained
½   cup brown sugar
1   tbsp. cornstarch
½   tsp. salt
1   cup orange juice
¼   cup golden raisins
2   tbsp. dry sherry
½   cup walnuts or pecans halved
½   tsp. orange peel, freshly grated

Preheat oven to 350°.

1. Bake potatoes in oven until done. Cool and peel.

2. Cut potatoes into ½" slices and place in buttered 9" x 13" casserole.

3. Combine remaining ingredients and pour mixture over potatoes. Bake 30 to 40 minutes.

This is a fast, easy and tasty casserole. Can be made ahead and refrigerated. Increase baking time to about an hour if casserole has been in refrigerator.

Myrtle and Art Burnett. Myrtle was born in 1918 in Coeur d'
Alene. She went to school there and walked 3.5 miles one way
to school. She graduated from high school in 1937 and went
to Whitney Business College. She worked with a mining company earning $20.00 a month. Later she worked for an insur-
ance company. She walked 7 miles a day to get to and from
work. Myrtle married Art in 1937 and had 2 girls and 5 boys.
Today they have 32 grandchildren, 44 great-grandchildren and
2 great-great grandchildren.

Robert Gunter Collection

Sweet Potatoes with Caramelized Apples
Serves eight to ten

6   sweet potatoes about 4 lbs.
1   tsp. salt
3   Granny Smith apples, peeled and cored
1   tbsp. fresh lemon juice
9   tbsp. butter unsalted plus more for pan
6   tbsp. brown sugar
6   tbsp. heavy cream
¼   cup *Calvados Brandy or regular brandy
¼   cup fresh orange juice

Preheat oven to 425°.

1. Bake potatoes until soft, 40 to 50 minutes. When cool enough to handle, peel and place flesh in medium bowl. Add salt and mash with fork.

2. Slice apples into one-eighth inch thick wedges and place in medium bowl. Add lemon juice and toss to combine.

3. In medium skillet, melt 3 tablespoons butter over medium high heat. Add 2 tablespoons brown sugar and cook, stirring until sugar dissolves. Cook apple slices in the butter and sugar in 3 or 4 batches. Cook until golden and caramelized, about 1 minute on each side. As they finish cooking, transfer to plate and set aside.

4. In a medium skillet, melt 3 tablespoons butter over high heat. Add 2 tablespoons brown sugar and cook until sugar dissolves.

5. Stir in 4 tablespoons cream, the Calvados or brandy and cook until slightly thickened, about 1 minute. Remove from heat and add to sweet potatoes, mixing well to combine.

6. Transfer potato mixture to a buttered 3 quart ovenproof casserole. Arrange apple slices over potatoes; set aside.

7. In medium skillet, melt remaining 3 tablespoons butter over medium heat. Add remaining 2 tablespoons brown sugar and cook until dissolved. Add remaining 2 tablespoons of cream and cook, stirring for 30 seconds.

8. Stir in orange juice and cook for 1 to 2 minutes, until thickened and dark brown. Pour over apples and cover with aluminum foil.

9. Bake until heated through, about 30 minutes.

Can serve immediately after removing from oven, or let stand at room temperature for up to 30 minutes before serving.

* Calvados is a French Apple Brandy.

The Best French Scalloped Potatoes
Serves six

2	tbsp. salted cold butter
2	lbs. Russet or Yukon Gold potatoes (about six medium) peeled and thinly sliced
1½	tsp. salt
1½	cups half and half
½	cup heavy cream

Preheat oven to 325°.

1. Rub 1 tablespoon of cold butter on bottom of 2 quart baking dish.

2. Overlay potatoes in 3 layers, sprinkling each layer with a little salt.

3. Pour half and half over potatoes. Use just enough to cover them.

4. Dot top with remaining butter.

5. Bake potatoes in middle of oven for 45 minutes.

6. Spoon heavy cream over top layer of potatoes and continue baking for another 45 minutes or until they are golden brown and have a light crust.

7. The potatoes will hold in warm oven until served.

No one knows how to scallop potatoes like the French. Double this elegant recipe because everyone loves it. Great served second day with quick warm-up.

Jim Parsons Jr. Collection

Vegetable Supreme
Serves six

2   8 oz. pkg. refrigerator crescent dinner roll dough
2   8 oz. packages cream cheese, softened
1   cup mayonnaise
1   pkg. Ranch dressing
3   cups finely chopped raw vegetables, use 4 or 5 kinds (see vegetable suggestions below)
1   cup Cheddar or Monterey Jack cheese, grated
½   cup Parmesan cheese, grated

Vegetable suggestions

mushrooms, squash, onions, tomatoes, broccoli, cauliflower, shredded carrot, green, yellow, or red peppers, peas

Preheat oven to 350°.

1. Press dough on large cookie sheet making a raised edge. Bake for 10 minutes. Cool to room temperature.

2. Combine cream cheese, mayonnaise and ranch dressing and mix well. Spread evenly on cooled crust. Gently press vegetables into mixture.

3. Top with cheeses. Refrigerate for at least one hour before cutting into squares or triangles.

If you are too busy to cook, let the kids cook this.

Winter Squash in Artichoke Bottoms

Serves eight

1½	lbs. acorn squash
¼	cup balsamic vinegar
2	tbsp. orange-flavored liqueur
1	shallot, chopped
1½	tsp. marjoram, dried
4	tbsp. butter, unsalted
¼	cup cream cheese
2	tbsp. poppy seeds
2	tbsp. brown sugar, packed
16	artichoke bottoms, cooked
	salt and pepper to taste

Preheat oven to 350°.

1. Cut squash, remove seeds and sprinkle squash with balsamic vinegar. Place on an ovenproof plate.

2. Cover with plastic wrap and microwave until tender (about 8 minutes).

3. Scoop cooked squash from the shell and place in a food processor. Add the remaining ingredients except the artichokes. Process well. Taste and adjust seasonings. Fill artichoke bottoms with the squash mixture.

4. Bake for about 10 minutes. (Or cover with plastic and heat in the microwave for about 5 minutes).

This is tasty and impressive as an appetizer or side dish.

273

Zucchini Baked Rice

Serves eight

1	cup rice, uncooked
3	medium zucchini, sliced
2	7½ oz. cans chopped green chilies
1½	cup grated jack cheese
2	large tomatoes, sliced
2	cups sour cream
1	tsp. oregano
1	tsp. garlic salt
¼	cup chopped green peppers
¼	cup chopped green onions
2	tbsp. chopped fresh parsley
	salt and pepper to taste

Preheat oven to 350°.

1. Cook rice according to standard directions. Cook zucchini until tender.

2. Butter a 9" x 13" casserole and place rice in bottom. Cover with green chilies and ¾ cup of jack cheese.

3. Cover with layer of zucchini and then sliced tomatoes. Salt and pepper to taste.

4. Mix sour cream, oregano, garlic salt, green pepper and green onions. Spoon mixture over tomatoes and sprinkle on the remaining jack cheese.

5. Bake for about 45 to 50 minutes. Sprinkle with parsley and serve.

Alpine Glow
Brendan Rodgers

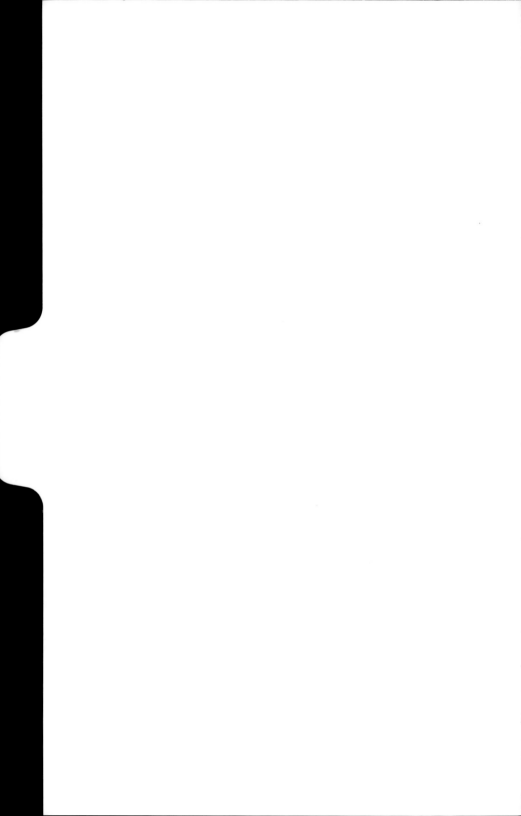

Desserts

Sadie Hadeen and Paul Tillberg, December 16, 1925
Mae Burt Collection

The Sadie and Paul Tillberg's children,1944: Paul Jr., Irma, Gloria, May, Morris, John. Front (L to R) Stan & Steve in basket.

Anise Almond Biscotti

Makes about 3 dozen

3¼	cups all-purpose flour
1	tbsp. baking powder
⅓	tsp. salt
1½	cups sugar
10	tbsp. unsalted butter, melted
3	large eggs
1	tbsp. vanilla extract
2	tsp. anise seed, ground
1	cup toasted whole almonds, coarsely chopped
1	large egg white

Preheat oven to 350°.

1. Position rack in center of oven. Line baking sheet with parchment paper.

2. Sift flour, baking powder and salt into medium bowl.

3. Mix sugar, melted butter, eggs, vanilla extract and ground anise seed in large bowl.

4. Add flour mixture to egg mixture and stir with wooden spoon until well blended. Mix in almonds.

5. Divide dough in half. Shape each half into a 13½" long, 2½" wide log. Transfer both logs to prepared baking sheet, spacing apart.

6. Whisk egg white in small bowl until foamy; brush over top and sides of each dough log.

7. Bake logs until golden brown (logs will spread), about 30 minutes. Cool logs completely on sheet on rack, about 25 minutes. Maintain oven temperature.

8. Transfer logs to work surface; discard parchment paper. Using serrated knife, cut logs on diagonal into ½" wide slices. Arrange slices, cut side down, on same baking sheet. Bake 12 minutes. Turn biscotti over; bake until just beginning to color, about 8 minutes. Transfer to rack and cool.

This is the traditional taste of Italy. Serve with morning coffee. Can be prepared 1 week ahead. Store in airtight container at room temperature.

Apple Bars

½   cup butter
1   cup sugar
1   beaten egg
½   cup chopped nuts
2   medium apples, peeled, cored and finely chopped
1   cup flour
½   tsp. baking powder
½   tsp. baking soda
½   tsp. salt
½   tsp. cinnamon

Preheat oven to 350°.

1. Cream butter, add sugar and beat in egg. Stir in nuts and chopped apples.

2. Sift dry ingredients together and fold into batter.

3. Turn batter into a greased 7" x 11" baking pan.

4. Bake for 40 minutes. Test with toothpick.

5. Cool and cut into squares.

This recipe freezes well.

Anton & Kristine Haugness married June 13, 1914. Parents of Dagmar Kirking on page 287. Dagmar and Marvin Kirking Collection

Aunt Mary's Sheet Cake

4	cups sifted flour
1	cup sugar
1	tsp. baking powder
1	tsp. baking soda
	pinch salt
¼	tsp. nutmeg
1	cup butter
1	cup sour cream
4	beaten egg yolks
6	oz. apricot, peach or seedless raspberry preserves
4	egg whites
2	tbsp. powdered sugar
1	tsp. vanilla
½	cup chopped nuts

Preheat oven to 350°.

1. Sift dry ingredients together.

2. Cut in butter as for pie dough. Make a well in dry mixture.

3. Blend egg yolks with sour cream and add to dry mixture. Mix well.

4. Pat into a buttered 10" x 15" cookie sheet.

5. Spread with preserve of your choice.

6. Beat egg whites stiff; fold in powdered sugar and vanilla. Spread on top of preserves.

7. Sprinkle with chopped nuts.

8. Place on low rack in oven and bake for 30 minutes. Low rack will brown dough but not burn meringue.

9. When cool, cut into diamond shapes. (Moisten knife with hot water to avoid sticking.)

Best Ever Pie Crust

Makes two crusts for a 9" pie

Liquid Mixture

1	beaten egg
5	tbsp. water
1	tbsp. vinegar

Dry Ingredients

3	cups flour
1	tsp. salt
1¼	cup vegetable shortening

1. Mix egg, water and vinegar in a cup and set aside.

2. In a large bowl, cut flour, salt and shortening with a pastry blender until mixture is well blended.

3. Pour liquid mixture over dry mixture and stir until blended. The dough will be sticky.

4. Overlap long edges of two 14" long pieces of wax paper about 2". Sprinkle surface lightly with flour.

5. Divide dough in half and place one-half in center of paper. Sprinkle top of dough lightly with flour. Place another piece of wax paper on top.

6. Roll out dough to fit 9" pie plate. Peel off top piece of wax paper. Place pie plate on top of crust and turn over. Repeat with remaining dough.

7. Peel off bottom piece of wax paper. Trim and crimp edges of crusts.

Don't skip the waxed paper; this makes an excellent crust, but the dough is sticky.

Bourbon Apple Pie

Serves six to eight

Pastry for double crust (See page 284.)

6-7	cups peeled Pippen or Granny Smith apples sliced ¼" thick
2	tbsp. bourbon
¾	cup sugar
2	tbsp. flour
1	tsp. cinnamon
¼	tsp. nutmeg
¼	tsp. salt
½	cup toasted pecans
½	cup bourbon, warmed
½	cup raisins soaked in bourbon
2	tbsp. butter
	milk and additional sugar for top

Preheat oven to 425°.

1. Combine sliced apples with 2 tablespoons bourbon and toss.

2. Combine sugar, flour, cinnamon, nutmeg and salt. Toss with apples.

3. Add toasted pecans and raisins that have been plumped in ½ cup warm bourbon. Pile into prepared pastry shell. Dot apples with pieces of butter. Top with pastry. Brush pastry top with milk and sprinkle with sugar.

4. Bake in lower third of oven for 50 to 60 minutes.

Burnt Cream
Serves Six

1	pint whipping cream
4	egg yolks
½	cup granulated sugar
1	tsp. vanilla

Preheat oven to 350°.

1. Heat cream over low heat until it bubbles around the edge of the pan.

2. Beat egg yolks and sugar together until thick and yellow. Beat constantly while pouring heated cream in a steady stream into the egg yolk/sugar mixture. Stir in vanilla.

3. Pour mixture into six 6 oz. custard cups or 4 oz. ramekins.

4. Place custard cups in a baking pan filled with 1" of boiling water.

5. Bake for 45 minutes. Remove cups and refrigerate until chilled (about 2 hours).

6. Sprinkle each custard cup with granulated sugar. Place cups on a pan and put them on oven rack closest to broiler. Broil, carefully, until sugar melts and turns medium brown.

7. Chill for an hour, then serve.

This impressive dessert is easy!

Dagmar Haugness and Marvin Kirking, November 15, 1952.
Parents on page 281. Dagmar Kirking Collection

Chocolate Angel Food Cake
with Hershey Almond Frosting
Serves ten to twelve

Cake batter

¾   cup cake flour
¼   cup cocoa
⅓   cup sugar
1½   cups egg whites
1½   tsp. cream of tartar
¼   tsp. salt
2   tsp. vanilla
¾   cup sugar

Frosting

10   oz. Hershey almond chocolate bar (1½ large
     bars)
3   cups whipping cream
¼   cup powdered sugar
1   tsp. vanilla

Preheat oven to 375°.

1. For cake batter sift first 3 ingredients together 4 times.

2. Put next 4 ingredients in mixer bowl, and beat at medium speed while adding sugar, two tablespoons at a time.

3. Increase speed, and continue beating until meringue holds stiff peaks. Remove from mixer and gradually fold in flour/sugar mixture until blended.

4. Push batter into ungreased 10" tube pan. Gently cut through batter with a knife. Bake for 35-40 minutes.

5. When cake tests done, invert pan and let hang upside down until cold. Split into two layers in preparation for frosting.

6. For frosting melt chocolate bar over hot water. Whip cream until stiff. Add powdered sugar and vanilla.

7. Gently fold melted chocolate into whipped cream mixture. Quickly frost bottom cake layer, then sides and top. Freeze immediately.

8. Thaw at room temperature for an hour or so before serving. Serve partially frozen with vanilla ice cream.

Chocolate Pecan Toffee Mousse Pie
Serves twelve to sixteen

Crust

½   lb. pecan pieces
¼   cup unsalted butter
¼   cup sugar
2   tbsp. water

Mousse

14 oz. semi-sweet chocolate
2   tbsp. vegetable oil
2   cups heavy whipping cream

Sauce

½   cup unsalted butter
¾   cup sugar
1   cup heavy cream

Preheat oven to 325°.

1. For crust grind pecans in food processor about 45 seconds and place in mixing bowl.

2. Melt butter in saucepan, add sugar, stirring constantly until mixture is a thick, smooth paste. Remove from heat and add water, stirring constantly to create syrup.

3. Pour over pecans and mix thoroughly.

4. Butter and flour a 12" spring form pan. Press pecan mixture into pan and bake for 10 minutes or until golden brown. Remove and let cool.

5. For mousse melt chocolate in a double boiler and add vegetable oil. Chocolate should be smooth and almost liquid.

6. Whip cream to form soft peaks. Add hot chocolate, stirring constantly until completely combined. (A slow speed mixer will do fine.) Pour into pie shell and refrigerate for 2 hours.

7. For sauce melt butter over medium high heat and add sugar. Stir frequently. Continue until mixture reaches a deep caramel color. Butter and sugar will separate; this is not a problem.

8. Remove from heat and slowly add heavy cream, stirring constantly. (Caution: when adding cream, mixture will bubble and release steam; use a whisk with a long handle or wear an oven mitt.)

9. After cream has been added, strain sauce into a container and let cool. Refrigerate. Reheat before serving.

10. Decorate with pecan halves. Cut pie into individual pieces and spoon toffee sauce over each serving.

Chocolate Peanut Ice Cream Dessert
Serves twelve to sixteen

¼   cup melted butter
2   cups crushed vanilla wafers
½   cup softened butter
2   cups powdered sugar
3   eggs
6   oz. chocolate chips, melted
2½   cups roasted chopped peanuts
1   quart vanilla ice cream

1. To prepare crust blend melted butter with crushed vanilla wafers and press into a 9" x 13" pan.

2. For filling mix softened butter with powdered sugar. Beat in eggs, one at a time. Add melted chocolate chips and 2 cups of roasted chopped peanuts.

3. Pour over base and freeze 30 minutes. Spread 1 quart slightly soft vanilla ice cream over all and sprinkle with remaining chopped nuts. Freeze.

4. Cut into squares and serve.

A crowd pleaser.

Chocolate Pound Cake

1 cup butter
½ cup shortening
3 cups sugar
5 eggs
½ tsp. salt
½ tsp. baking powder
3 cups flour
½ cup cocoa
1 cup milk
2 tsp. vanilla

Preheat oven to 300°.

1. Cream butter, shortening and sugar. Add eggs one at a time and beat well.

2. Sift dry ingredients together and add alternately with milk and vanilla.

3. Bake in greased tube pan for 1 hour 30 minutes or until done.

Christmas Plum Pudding
Serves six to eight

3	cups whole wheat bread crumbs
½	cup sugar
½	cup melted butter
1	large egg, beaten
⅓	cup milk
1	tsp. baking soda
⅓	cup strong coffee
½	cup brandy
1	cup currants
1	cup raisins
1	cup chopped walnuts
3	tsp. cinnamon
½	tsp. cloves

1. Freeze bread. Cut off crusts and use grater to make crumbs.

2. Mix together all ingredients in large bowl.

3. Pour into well-buttered pudding mold with a lid.

4. Set on rack in deep kettle. Fill kettle with boiling water halfway up side of pudding mold.

5. Cover kettle and steam over low heat for 3 or 4 hours, adding boiling water as needed. Serve with fresh thick cream.

This recipe came from London in 1972. It has been changed over the years and still remains a favorite Yuletide treat. Make several up to two months ahead to give as gifts.

Coconut Custard Pie

Serves eight

2	cups milk
1	cup sugar
½	cup softened butter
½	cup flour
¼	tsp. vanilla
1	egg
1	cup shredded coconut

Preheat oven to 350°.

1. Mix first six ingredients in a blender. Add coconut and mix by hand.

2. Pour into a 10" buttered, glass pie pan (makes own crust).

3. Bake for 40-45 minutes.

4. Cool completely before cutting.

Cracker Nut Pie

Serves six to eight

20	thin saltines (double crackers)
1¼	tsp. baking powder
4	egg whites
1⅓	cups sugar
1	tsp. vanilla
1	cup chopped pecans
1	cup heavy cream, whipped
	strawberries for decoration

Preheat oven to 350°.

1. Crush crackers into fine crumbs. Use a rolling pin or blender.

2. Add baking powder, mix well and set aside.

3. Beat egg whites until stiff but not dry. Gradually beat in sugar until stiff. Gently fold in vanilla, pecans and crumbs. Mix gently but well.

4. Pour into a well-greased 9" pan.

5. Bake for 30 minutes or until golden brown and firm. Cool.

6. Garnish with whipped cream and strawberries.

Cranberry Pecan Bars
Makes three dozen bars

Crust
1	cup flour
2	tbsp. sugar
⅓	cup butter
½	cup chopped pecans

Filling
1¼	cups sugar
2	tbsp. flour
2	beaten eggs
2	tbsp. milk
1	tbsp. grated orange peel
1	tsp. vanilla
½	cup chopped pecans
1	cup fresh cranberries, chopped

Preheat oven to 350°.

1. To prepare crust, mix flour, sugar and cut in butter. Add pecans. Press into ungreased 9" x 13" pan. Bake for 15 minutes. Cool.

2. Mix filling ingredients together. Spread over cooled, partially baked crust. Bake for 25 to 30 minutes or until top is golden.

3. Cut into 36 bars while still warm. Cool completely before serving.

This is a delicious holiday treat. For variation add ½ cup of coconut to filling.

Cranberry Orange Pound Cake
Serves sixteen

Batter

1	pkg. yellow cake mix
1	4 oz. pkg. vanilla instant pudding mix
1	cup water
½	cup melted butter
1-2	tsp. fresh grated orange peel
4	eggs
1½	cups fresh or frozen cranberries (unthawed)

Sauce

1	cup sugar
1-2	tbsp. flour
½	cup orange juice
½	cup butter

Preheat oven to 350°.

1. Beat dry cake mix, pudding mix, water, butter, orange peel and eggs in large bowl with an electric mixer on low speed for 30 seconds. Continue to beat on medium speed for 2 minutes.

2. Fold in cranberries and spread mixture in a buttered Bundt pan.

3. Bake 1 hour and 5 minutes or until cake springs back when touched gently in center. Cool 10 minutes and remove from pan.

4. For sauce mix sugar and flour in a saucepan. Stir in orange juice. Add butter and cook over medium heat. Stir constantly until thickened. Pour warm sauce over cake. Garnish with cranberries and holly.

Cream Sherry Dessert
Serves eight

½	cup cream sherry
1	envelope gelatin
3	egg yolks
½	cup sugar
3	egg whites
1	cup whipping cream
1½	cups chocolate cookie wafer crumbs
4	tbsp. melted butter

1. Heat sherry to just below boiling point. Dissolve gelatin in sherry and cool.

2. In large bowl, beat egg yolks until light; gradually add sugar, beating well. Add to sherry/gelatin mixture. Beat egg whites until stiff. Beat whipping cream. Fold both into the sherry mixture.

3. For crust mix together cookie crumbs and melted butter and press into 11" x 7" pan, saving ½ cup mixture for top. Spread sherry mixture over crumb layer and top with remaining crumbs.

4. Refrigerate 4 – 6 hours or overnight.

Try this easy and delicious dessert. In the summer, dress it up with flowers.

Creole Bread Pudding
Serves twelve

Bread Pudding

3	eggs
1¼	cups sugar
2	tsp. vanilla
½	tsp. cinnamon
½	tsp. nutmeg
4	tbsp. melted butter
1	quart whole milk
1	cup raisins
½	cup chopped pecans, lightly toasted
1	loaf sweet French bread, cubed

Bourbon Whiskey Sauce

2	cups water
1¼	cups sugar
2	tbsp. butter
½	tsp. cinnamon
½	tsp. nutmeg
2	tbsp. cornstarch
¼	cup bourbon

Preheat oven to 350°.

1. Beat eggs with mixer about 3 minutes. Add sugar, vanilla, cinnamon, nutmeg and butter until well blended. Mix in milk, raisins and pecans.

2. Add bread cubes and let sit for about 30 minutes, patting bread down occasionally. Pour into greased shallow baking pan and smooth top. Bake for 45 minutes or until set.

3. For sauce combine water, sugar, butter, cinnamon and nutmeg in a saucepan. Bring to boil. Mix bourbon and cornstarch; add to mixture. Cook, stirring until thickened.

4. Serve pudding with warm whiskey sauce.

Divine Caramel Pecan Cheesecake
Serves ten to twelve

Crust

14	graham crackers (double crackers)
⅓	cup firmly packed brown sugar
½	cup pecans
⅓	cup melted butter

Filling

1	14 oz. can sweetened condensed milk
½	cup toffee bits (Skor or Heath)
3	8 oz. pkgs. cream cheese
½	cup firmly packed brown sugar
4	large eggs

Ganache

½	cup heavy cream
2	tbsp. unsalted butter
4	oz. semisweet chocolate, finely chopped

Preheat oven to 350°.

1. For crust combine the crackers, sugar and pecans in a food processor fitted with chopping blade. Mix until combined. Add butter in a thin stream until well mixed.

2. Place mixture in bottom of a 10" spring form pan and press firmly. Bake for 15 minutes. Remove from oven and cool. Turn oven down to 325°.

3. Combine sweetened condensed milk and toffee

bits in small saucepan. Bring to a boil over low to medium heat, stirring frequently until milk reaches a pale brown color and smells like caramel. Cool.

4. Combine cream cheese, caramelized milk and sugar. Beat until smooth. Add eggs, one at a time, mixing well after each addition.

5. Pour over crust. Bake for 45 minutes to 1 hour until filling is set. Cool.

6. For ganache bring cream and butter to a simmer in small saucepan. Remove from heat, add chocolate and cover for 5 minutes. Remove lid and stir until smooth. Cool slightly and pour over cooled filling.

Dried Fruit Cordial
Makes 1½ quarts

1	lb. dried fruit (apricots, prunes with pits, pears or peaches)
1	bottle (4/5 quart) or 3½ cups dry white wine
1	cup brandy
2	cups sugar

1. Place dried fruit in glass container. Stir in wine, brandy and sugar until well blended.

2. Cover tightly. Let stand at room temperature for at least one week to allow flavors to develop. Stir occasionally the first few days until sugar is dissolved.

3. After one week fruit should be slightly firm. Fruit flavor of wine reaches maximum intensity in 3 or 4 weeks. After about six weeks, if fruit becomes too soft, remove it; wine keeps indefinitely.

4. Can serve cordial with a piece of marinated fruit. Also use fruit from cordial as an ice cream topping.

Fruit cordials make a special gift. Repack in small containers with tight fitting lids.

John D. and Minnie Dobroth, March 14, 1913.
Attendants Carl and Ann Carlson. Walter Burt Collection

Flourless Chocolate Cake

Serves eight to ten

Batter

8	oz. European semi-sweet chocolate
1	cup unsalted butter
5	eggs
1⅓	cups sugar
2	tbsp. flour
1	tbsp. vanilla
¼	tsp. salt

Ganache

¼	cup heavy cream
1	tbsp. unsalted butter
1½	tsp. light corn syrup
3	oz. European bittersweet chocolate

Preheat oven to 325°.

1. In saucepan melt chocolate and butter. Remove from heat and cool.

2. In large bowl whisk eggs with sugar, flour, vanilla and salt. Add cooled chocolate and butter.

3. Grease and flour sides of an 8" or 9" pan. Line bottom of pan with waxed paper.

4. Bake for 70 minutes. Remove from oven, transfer to a rack and peel off wax paper. (This will be a rich moist almost pudding type cake.)

5. For ganache bring to a boil the cream, butter, light corn syrup and bittersweet chocolate. Let cool.

6. Spread ganache on cool cake.

Can use 2 oz. melted white chocolate for design on top.

This elegant and rich dessert will highlight any festive meal.

Frosty Berry Dessert

Serves ten to twelve

Crust

1	cup flour
¼	cup brown sugar
½	cup chopped walnuts
½	cup melted butter

Filling

2	egg whites
1	cup sugar
2	cups fresh sliced strawberries **or** fresh raspberries **or** 1 ten oz. box frozen (Can use either strawberries or raspberries.)
2	tbsp. lemon juice
1	cup whipping cream, whipped

Topping

fresh berries for decoration

Prepare at least 6 hours ahead of serving.

Preheat oven to 350°.

1. Combine flour, brown sugar, walnuts and melted butter in 13" x 9" baking pan. Bake for 20 minutes, stirring occasionally. Cool. Sprinkle ⅔ of this crumb mixture in a 13" x 9" pan. Save remaining crumbs for topping.

2. For filling, combine egg whites, sugar, sliced strawberries and lemon juice. Beat at high speed in mixer until stiff peaks form, about 10 minutes. (Keep beating; it will get stiff.)

3. Fold in whipped cream and spoon over crumbs in pan. Top with reserved crumbs.

4. Freeze 6 hours or overnight.

5. Cut into squares and garnish with whole berries.

This excellent dessert will last 4 weeks in the freezer. It is easy to cut, and the taste is elegant and smooth. People will want seconds!

Fudge Upside Down Cake
Serves eight to ten

Batter

2	cups flour
¼	cup unsweetened cocoa powder
4	tsp. baking powder
½	tsp. salt
1⅔	cups granulated sugar
1	cup chopped walnuts
1	cup milk, room temperature
¼	cup melted butter
2	tsp. vanilla
1	oz. unsweetened chocolate, melted

Sauce

1	cup granulated sugar
1	cup brown sugar, packed
½	cup plus 2 tbsp. unsweetened cocoa powder
1¾	cups hot water

Preheat oven to 325°.

1. To prepare batter sift flour, cocoa, baking powder and salt into large bowl. Mix in sugar and nuts.

2. Whisk milk, butter and vanilla in medium bowl. Add to dry ingredients and beat well. Beat in chocolate. Spoon batter into a buttered 9" x 13" pan and set aside.

3. For sauce mix both sugars and cocoa in medium bowl. Gradually add hot water and stir until smooth.

4. Gently pour sauce over back of spoon onto cake batter covering batter completely.

5. Bake about 50 minutes. The cake will be firm to touch and top browned. Let cool slightly.

6. To serve, cut cake while still warm. Spoon fudge sauce from baking pan over cake. Best if served warm.

This is a very rich cake and just begs to be served with ice cream.

Huckleberry Apple Pie
with Streusel Topping
Serves eight

9" uncooked pie crust. See page 284.

Filling

5	cups tart apples, pared and thinly sliced
1	cup huckleberries (blueberries may be substituted)
¾	cup granulated sugar
¼	cup all-purpose flour
½	tsp. freshly grated nutmeg
¾	tsp. ground cinnamon

Topping

8	tbsp. firm butter
1	cup all-purpose flour
½	cup brown sugar, packed

Preheat oven to 375°.

1. Fit pastry into a 9" pie plate and flute edges.

2. Combine filling ingredients and spoon into pie shell.

3. For topping cut butter into flour with a pastry blender until crumbly. Toss with brown sugar. Sprinkle topping over pie filling.

4. Bake for 50-60 minutes. Cover with foil last 10 minutes if top browns too quickly.

Huckleberry Cream Cheese Pastry

1   pkg. refrigerated crescent rolls
4   oz. cream cheese
1   tbsp. lemon juice
3-4   tbsp. sugar
½-¾   cup huckleberries

Preheat oven to 375°.

1. Roll out and make square of ½ of crescent roll dough.

2. Place half of dough on a cookie sheet. Make certain there are no holes in dough.

3. Mix cream cheese, lemon juice, and sugar together and spread on dough.

4. Sprinkle berries over cream cheese mixture.

5. Cover berries with other half of dough. Pinch edges together. Perforations in dough will be vent holes.

6. Bake for about 15 minutes or until pastry is browned.

You may want to add more berries and sugar to make the cream cheese filling thicker.

313

Lemon Cloud Pie
Serves eight

Crust

1	cup flour
½	tsp. salt
⅓	cup shortening
1	slightly beaten egg
1	tsp. grated lemon rind
1	tbsp. fresh lemon juice

Filling

1	cup sugar
¼	cup cornstarch
1	cup water
1	tsp. grated lemon rind
⅓	cup fresh lemon juice
2	eggs, separated
4	oz. cream cheese

Preheat oven to 425°.

1. To prepare pie crust sift together flour and salt. Cut shortening into flour. Combine egg, lemon rind and lemon juice; mix with flour/shortening.

2. Roll out crust for a single 9" pie. Bake about 12 minutes until golden.

3. For filling combine sugar, cornstarch, water, lemon rind and lemon juice in a saucepan. Cook over medium heat until mixture begins to thicken.

4. Mix a small amount of hot mixture with slightly beaten egg yolks, and then add back into hot

314

mixture.

5. When thick, remove from heat, add cream cheese and blend well.

6. Beat egg whites until stiff; fold into lemon/cream cheese mixture. Pour into baked pie shell.

This pie is a long-time family favorite!

Lime Pineapple Torte

Serves twenty

1	cup sifted flour
1	cup sugar
½	cup butter or margarine
½	cup chopped nuts
1	1 lb. 4½ oz. can crushed pineapple
1	3 oz. pkg. lime gelatin
1	8 oz. pkg. cream cheese or light cream cheese (not non-fat), softened
¼	tsp. peppermint extract
⅔	cup heavy cream

Chocolate Glaze

1	cup semisweet chocolate pieces (one 6 oz. pkg.)
2	tbsp. butter or margarine
⅔	cup heavy cream
¼	tsp. peppermint extract

Preheat oven to 400°.

1. Combine flour and ¼ cup sugar. Cut butter into mixture until it resembles cornmeal. Add nuts.

2. Press mixture into bottom of 9" x 13" pan and bake for 15 minutes. Cool.

3. Drain pineapple reserving 1 cup of syrup.

4. Heat syrup to a boil. Pour over gelatin and stir to dissolve. Cool slightly.

5. Combine softened cream cheese and remaining sugar and beat until light and fluffy.

6. Gradually add gelatin mixture and beat until blended.

7. Stir in pineapple and peppermint extract. Chill until partially set.

8. Whip cream until stiff and fold into partially set gelatin mixture. Turn into baked crust and chill.

9. For chocolate glaze combine chocolate, butter and cream in a saucepan. Cook and stir over low heat until smooth. Stir in peppermint extract. Cool.

10. Drizzle chocolate glaze over the top of partially set torte and chill at least 4 hours.

If you prefer a solid chocolate top to the drizzled one, double or triple the recipe for the glaze. This is a lovely dessert for Christmas or St. Patrick's Day because of the green color. Garnish it with mint leaves or lime slices. After the torte has chilled, precut or at least score it into serving pieces.

Madeleines
Makes about twenty

2   large eggs
⅔   cup sugar
2   tsp. vanilla
½   tsp. grated lemon peel
       pinch salt
1   cup flour
10   tbsp. unsalted butter, melted, cooled slightly
       powdered sugar

Preheat oven to 375°.

1. Generously butter and flour pan for large madeleines (about 3" x 1¼") *

2. Using electric mixer blend eggs and sugar in a large bowl. Beat in vanilla, lemon peel and salt. Add flour; beat just until blended.

3. Gradually add cooled butter and beat just until blended.

4. Spoon 1 tablespoon batter into each indentation in pan. Bake until puffed and brown, about 13 minutes. Cool and gently remove from pan.

5. Repeat process. Butter and flour pan before each batch.

6. Dust cookies with powdered sugar.

* A metal mold with scallop-shaped indentations available at cookware stores.

Mandarin Orange Cake
Serves eight

Cake

1	cup sugar
1	cup flour
½	tsp. salt
1	tsp. soda
1	beaten egg
1	tsp. vanilla
1	11 oz. can mandarin oranges, juice and all

Topping

3	tbsp. butter
¾	cup brown sugar
3	tbsp. milk

Preheat oven 350°.

1. Mix dry ingredients in medium sized bowl.

2. In separate bowl, mix egg and vanilla, then add entire can of mandarin oranges, including juice.

3. Add egg mixture to dry ingredients; stir until moistened. Pour into a greased 8" x 8" pan.

4. Bake for 30 minutes.

5. For topping melt butter in saucepan. Stir in brown sugar and then milk until well mixed. Bring to boil.

6. Remove from heat and pour over warm or cool cake.

Serve with whipped cream.

Marshmallows for Grown-Ups

3	pkg. unflavored gelatin
1	cup water
1½	cups granulated sugar
1	cup light corn syrup
¼	tsp. sea/kosher salt
¼	tsp. mint flavoring
½	tsp. vanilla
3-4	drops green food coloring
	powdered sugar for dusting
	chocolate sprinkles

1. Combine gelatin and ½ cup cold water. Use bowl of electric mixer fitted with whisk attachment.

2. Combine sugar, corn syrup, salt and ½ cup water in a small pan. Cook over medium heat until sugar is dissolved. Continue cooking on high heat until syrup reaches 240° on a candy thermometer.

3. With mixer on slow speed, slowly pour syrup into dissolved gelatin. Increase speed to high and beat until very thick, about 15 minutes.

4. Add mint, vanilla and green food coloring and mix thoroughly.

5. With sieve dust an 8" x 8" baking dish with powdered sugar. Pour in marshmallow mixture and smooth the top. Add chocolate sprinkles.

6. Let stand overnight or until mixture dries out. Turn out onto a board and cut into small squares. Dust side with more powdered sugar.

Molasses Cookies

Makes four dozen

1½	cups oil
1	cup dark brown sugar
1	cup granulated sugar
½	cup Grandma's Molasses
2	eggs
4	cups unsifted flour (add 2 tablespoons more if needed)
2	tsp. baking soda
1	tsp. ground cloves
1	tsp. ginger
2	tsp. cinnamon
1	tsp. salt
	pinch allspice
	granulated sugar for the cookie dough balls

Preheat oven to 375°.

1. With an electric mixer, mix oil, sugars, molasses and eggs. Beat well. Sift dry ingredients together and add to molasses mixture; mix well. Chill thoroughly.

2. Form into 1" balls, roll in granulated sugar, and place on greased cookie sheet two inches apart.

3. Bake for 8 to 10 minutes. Watch carefully. Don't let them get too brown.

Cool on cooling racks, and store in airtight containers.

Molasses Lace Cookies
Makes four dozen

¾	cup sugar
½	cup molasses
⅓	cup water
¾	cup butter or margarine
1¼	cup flour
1½	tsp. baking powder
1¼	tsp. cinnamon
1	cup chopped nuts

Preheat oven to 325°.

1. Combine sugar, molasses, water and butter in a large saucepan. Heat just to boiling.

2. Remove from heat and stir until butter melts.

3. Sift dry ingredients together and add to molasses mixture. Fold in nuts. Let batter cool.

4. Drop batter by teaspoon on a greased cookie sheet. Place about 3" apart.

5. Bake for about 12 minutes or longer for crisper cookie. Let cool for about a minute and remove with a spatula before they harden. Cool completely on waxed paper.

Circa 1910
Jim Parsons Jr. Collection

Nemesis Au Chocolat

Serves sixteen

1½	cups sugar
½	cup water
2	tbsp. vanilla extract
8	oz. unsweetened chocolate, finely chopped
4	oz. bittersweet chocolate, finely chopped
1	cup unsalted butter cut into pieces, at room temperature
5	large eggs, room temperature

Preheat oven to 350°. May be prepared one day ahead.

1. Bring 1 cup sugar, water, and vanilla to a boil in heavy saucepan. Remove from heat. Add half unsweetened and bittersweet chocolate. Stir until smooth.

2. Whisk in half the butter. Add remaining chocolate and butter; whisk until smooth.

3. In large bowl using electric mixer, beat eggs with remaining sugar until pale yellow, and until slowly dissolving ribbons form when beaters are lifted. Beat in melted chocolate mixture.

4. Pour batter into a greased 9" diameter cake pan with bottom lined with wax paper. Place cake pan into larger baking pan. Add enough boiling water to baking pan to come halfway up sides of cake pan.

5. Bake until cake remains firm in center when shaken (about 30 minutes).

6. Remove cake from water. Cool 10 minutes. Unmold the cake onto plate. Cool completely.

7. Top with Crème Anglaise or Raspberry Sauce.

Raspberry Sauce

1	12 oz. bag of frozen raspberries
⅓	cup water
¼	cup plus 2 tbsp. orange juice
2	tbsp. sugar
2	tbsp. cornstarch
2	tbsp. seedless raspberry jam

1. Pureé raspberries with water and ¼ cup orange juice in food processor. Strain raspberry mixture through a sieve into a heavy saucepan. Mix in sugar.

2. Combine cornstarch and remaining orange juice in small bowl and mix until smooth. Add to raspberry mixture, stir while bringing to a boil. Mix in jam, cover and refrigerate until cool.

Crème Anglaise

⅔	cup sugar
6	egg yolks
2	cups milk
½	tsp. vanilla

1. With mixer beat sugar and yolks in small bowl.

2. Scald milk in heavy saucepan over medium heat.

3. Gradually beat hot milk into yolks. Return to saucepan and heat; stir until mixture coats spoon, about 8 minutes. Do not boil. Strain into bowl and mix in vanilla. Cool. Cover and refrigerate.

Oatmeal Cake
Serves twelve to sixteen

Batter

1¼	cups boiling water
1	cup quick oats
½	cup butter
1	cup white sugar
1	cup brown sugar
2	eggs
1⅓	cups flour
½	tsp. salt
1	tsp. cinnamon
½	tsp. nutmeg

Topping

6	tbsp. butter
¼	cup cream or whole milk
½	cup sugar
½	tsp. vanilla
1	cup nuts (walnuts)
1	cup flake coconut

Preheat oven to 350°.

1. Pour boiling water over quick oats and butter. Cover and let stand 20 minutes.

2. Add white sugar, brown sugar, eggs, flour, salt, cinnamon and nutmeg. Stir (don't over beat).

3. Grease and flour 9" x 13" cake pan.

4. Pour batter into pan and bake for 35 minutes or until toothpick comes out clean.

5. For topping combine butter, cream, sugar, vanilla, nuts and coconut in a sauce pan and bring to a boil. Stir constantly.

6. Spread over warm cake and broil until light brown and bubbly, about 5 minutes.

This is a fantastic dessert for anytime or any occasion.

Oatmeal Cookies "Rocks"

3	cups old-fashioned oatmeal uncooked
3	cups flour
1	cup chopped raisins
1½	cups brown sugar
½	cup white sugar
2	tsp. cinnamon
2	tsp. baking powder
1	cup chopped walnuts
1	cup melted butter
½	cup milk
3	beaten eggs

Preheat oven to 375°.

1. Mix all dry ingredients together. Add everything else. Mix well.

2. Refrigerate overnight.

3. Drop by teaspoons on greased baking sheet. Bake at 375° for 15 to 20 minutes.

4. Cool upside down on paper towels and store in a cookie jar.

These "Rocks" were made during WWI and shipped to the troops overseas. They have a marvelous keeping ability and are excellent for dunking.

Peach Buckle
Serves six

3   cups sliced peaches
1   cup sugar
¾   cup flour
¼   tsp. salt
¼   tsp. nutmeg or cinnamon
1½   tsp. baking powder
6   tbsp. butter
¾   cup milk
⅓   cup sliced almonds, optional

Preheat oven to 350°.

1. Stir together peaches and ¼ cup of sugar. In another bowl, mix flour, salt, nutmeg and baking powder with ¾ cup sugar. Slowly stir in milk.

2. Melt butter in an 8" baking pan or deep-dish pie tin. Tilt baking pan to spread butter evenly over entire inside surface.

3. Pour batter into pan. Spread but do not stir. Spoon peaches and almonds over batter.

4. Bake for 50 minutes or until top is evenly browned. Do not under bake.

Peach Spice Cake
Serves twelve

2	cups sugar
1	cup oil
2	eggs
4¼	cups sifted flour
2	tsp. soda
1	tsp. salt
1	tsp. nutmeg
1	tsp. cloves
1	tsp. allspice
1	tsp. cinnamon
1	cup chopped nuts
1	large can sliced peaches with juice

Preheat oven to 375°.

1. Cream sugar and oil; add eggs and beat.

2. Sift dry ingredients except nuts together.

3. Add dry ingredients and peaches alternately to sugar/oil/egg mixture.

4. Stir in nuts.

5. Bake in an ungreased tube pan for one hour and 20 minutes.

This is an excellent gift that keeps well and has a million dollar taste.

Peanut Butter Cup Bars

10   graham crackers (double crackers)
1   cup butter or margarine, softened
4   cups powdered sugar
1   cup peanut butter
2   cups chocolate chips (one 12 oz. pkg.)

1. Finely crush graham crackers.

2. Combine all ingredients except chocolate chips and mix well by hand.

3. Press dough into a 9" x 9" inch pan.

4. Melt chocolate chips and spread over top of dough.

5. Cool to room temperature, and cut into bars.

Peanut Butter Cup Bars are a fantastic treat for everyone who loves chocolate and peanut butter. And who doesn't?!

331

Pear Custard Bars

Makes sixteen bars

Crust

⅓   cup butter or margarine, softened
¼   cup sugar
⅓   cup all-purpose flour
¼   tsp. vanilla extract

Filling

1   8 oz. pkg. Neufchatel or cream cheese, softened
⅓   cup sugar
1   egg
½   tsp. vanilla extract
2   ripe pears, cored and thinly sliced (or use canned)
½   tsp. sugar
½   tsp. cinnamon

Preheat oven to 350°.

1. For crust combine butter and sugar; beat in flour and vanilla until combined. Press into a greased 8" square pan. Bake for 20 minutes. Cool.

2. For the filling, increase oven temperature to 375°. Beat cream cheese until smooth. Add sugar, egg and vanilla, and mix well. Pour over crust.

3. Arrange pear slices in single layer over filling. Combine sugar and cinnamon, and sprinkle over pears. Bake for 28-30 minutes. Cool and refrigerate for at least two hours before cutting. Cut into 16 bars and serve.

Pears Poached in Red Wine
Serves four to eight

4-8	pears
1	lemon
½	cup brown sugar
1	bottle burgundy wine (750 ml.)
4	cloves
1	vanilla bean

1. Juice lemon. Pour lemon juice into bowl or casserole large enough to accommodate all the pears. Add enough water so pears will be covered with the lemon/water bath.

2. Peel pears. As each one is finished, put it into lemon/water bath. Cover.

3. While pears are soaking, prepare wine mixture: Simmer wine, sugar and spices for 10 minutes. Remove pears from lemon/water bath and add to wine poaching liquid. Bring to boil. Turn pears. After 10 minutes, remove from heat. Cool to room temperature.

4. Refrigerate pears in liquid until ready to serve.

5. Serve with ice cream and/or pound cake.

333

Pennsylvania Dutch Peach Chiffon Pie
Serves eight

1	prebaked single pie crust (See page 284.)
1½	cups sliced, chopped fresh peaches
¾	cup granulated sugar
1	tbsp. lemon juice
1	tbsp. unflavored gelatin
¼	cup cold water
½	cup boiling water
½	cup whipping cream

1. Combine peaches and sugar. Let stand 20-30 minutes. Add lemon juice.

2. Soften gelatin in cold water. After 5 minutes add boiling water. Add to peaches and cool.

3. Beat whipping cream to stiff peak. Fold small amount of cream into peaches, then fold peaches into remaining cream.

4. Pour into pie crust and refrigerate.

Ella Farmin, circa 1910
The Robert Gunter Collection

Pink Grapefruit Chiffon Pie
Serves eight

1	pre-baked 9" single pie crust. (See page 284.)
1	medium sized pink grapefruit
1	envelope unflavored gelatin
1½	cups fresh pink grapefruit juice
3	eggs, separated
¾	cup sugar
¼	tsp. salt
¼	tsp. grated lemon peel, fresh or dried
¼	cup lemon juice
½	tsp. grated pink grapefruit peel (may substitute dry orange peel)
	red food coloring
¼	tsp. cream of tartar

Topping

sweetened whipped cream (optional)

1. Remove peel and white membrane from grapefruit; lift out sections and drain well.

2. Soften gelatin in 1 cup grapefruit juice.

3. Beat egg yolks and combine in a pan with remaining grapefruit juice, ½ cup sugar, salt, lemon peel, lemon juice and grapefruit peel.

4. Cook over low heat, stirring constantly, until mixture bubbles and lightly coats a metal spoon. Remove from heat, add softened gelatin, and stir until gelatin is completely dissolved.

5. Add a few drops food coloring to tint to a medium pink. Chill gelatin mixture until thick enough to mound on a spoon.

6. Beat 3 egg whites with cream of tartar until frothy (a little on the dry side); add remaining ¼ cup sugar and continue beating until stiff peaks form.

7. Beat gelatin mixture until light and frothy. Fold in grapefruit sections, reserving several for garnish; then fold in beaten egg whites. Spread in a pie crust, chill until firm, several hours or overnight.

Garnish with reserved grapefruit sections and dollops of whipped cream if desired.

This is a light and refreshing pie with a remarkable flavor. Think summer!

Rhubarb Custard Crisp
Serves eight to ten

3	eggs
2	tbsp. plus 2 tsp. milk (a little less than 3 tbsp.)
2	cups sugar
¼	cup flour
¾	tsp. nutmeg
4	cups diced rhubarb
1	tbsp. butter

Topping

¾	cup flour
½	cup ice cold butter, cut up
1	tbsp. cinnamon
¾	cup oatmeal, uncooked
½	cup dark brown sugar

Preheat oven to 375°.

1. For filling beat eggs and add milk.

2. Mix together sugar, flour, nutmeg and stir into egg mixture.

3. Mix in rhubarb. Pour into casserole or a 8" baking dish and dot with butter.

4. For topping use pastry blade in food processor and mix together flour, butter and cinnamon. Pour into a bowl and add oatmeal and brown sugar.

5. Crumble topping with your fingers. Pour over rhubarb filling and bake for 40 to 45 minutes.

6. Serve with cream.

Royal Rhubarb Crunch
Serves four to six

4   cups rhubarb, cut into 2" pieces

Syrup

1   cup sugar
1   cup water
1   tsp. vanilla
2   tbsp. cornstarch

Crunch

1   cup flour
¾   cup oatmeal
½   cup melted margarine or butter
1   cup brown sugar
1   tsp. cinnamon

Preheat oven to 350°.

1. For syrup mix together sugar, water, vanilla and cornstarch, and cook until thick. Set aside.

2. For crunch mix dry ingredients and add melted butter. Pat ½ of mixture into a 8" x 8" pan. Add rhubarb. Pour syrup over rhubarb. Add remaining crunch mixture to form upper crust. Bake for one hour.

3. Serve with ice cream or whipped cream.

Double recipe for 9" x 13" pan. This is the absolute superb rhubarb dessert.

Strawberry Cloud Soufflé with Chocolate Berry Garnish

Serves six to eight

2	pints hulled strawberries
2	envelopes unflavored gelatin
¾	cup cold water
¼	cup Kirsch liqueur
2	tbsp. sugar
1	tbsp. fresh lemon juice
4	egg whites at room temperature
¼	tsp. salt
¼	cup sugar
1	cup heavy cream, whipped

Garnish

1	pint strawberries
6	oz. semi-sweet melted chocolate

1. Pureé strawberries in a food processor. Set aside.

2. In a small saucepan sprinkle gelatin over water and stir over low heat until dissolved. Allow liquid to cool slightly.

3. Mix gelatin with strawberry pureé and stir in Kirsch, 2 tablespoons sugar and lemon juice.

4. Chill until slightly thickened but not set.

5. Beat egg whites and salt to soft peaks. Gradually beat in ¼ cup sugar and continue to beat until stiff, but not dry.

6. Fold strawberry mixture into whites; then fold in whipped cream.

7. Pour into buttered 1 quart soufflé dish fitted with a lightly buttered foil collar extending 2" over the rim. For best results the collar should be 3 layers thick. Individual soufflé dishes with collars may be used.

8. Chill several hours.

9. For garnish insert bamboo skewers into stem end of dry berries. Swirl in chocolate to cover ⅔ of the berries. Stand skewers in drinking glass until chocolate has hardened or about an hour.

10. Remove skewers and place strawberries on soufflé.

This elegant dessert is perfect for a luncheon. Can use wine goblets instead of soufflé dishes and collars. A dollop of whipped cream and a mint leaf make a nice touch.

Spicy Raisin Walnut Pie
Serves eight

1	unbaked 9" pie crust. (See page 284.)
3	eggs
⅔	cup sugar
½	tsp. salt
½	tsp. cinnamon
½	tsp. nutmeg
½	tsp. cloves
1	cup dark or light corn syrup
½	cup walnuts
½	cup raisins

Preheat oven to 375°.

1. With mixer, beat all ingredients except nuts and raisins.

2. After filling is well mixed, stir in nuts and raisins.

3. Pour into unbaked pie crust and bake 40-50 minutes until filling is set.

Also would make wonderful small tarts.

Ultimate Meyer Lemon Bars

Makes eighteen bars

2	cups sifted flour
½	cup sifted powdered sugar
1	cup butter
4	beaten eggs
2	cups granulated sugar
1	tsp. vanilla
⅓	cup Meyer lemon juice (Use regular lemons if Meyer lemons are not available.)
2	tsp. Meyer lemon zest
2	tbsp. melted butter
½	cup toasted coconut
½	cup dried cherries
⅓	cup flour
½	tsp. baking powder

Preheat oven to 350°.

1. Sift first two ingredients together. Cut in butter and mix until crumbly. Press into a 9" x 13"baking dish.

2. Bake for 20-25 minutes or until lightly browned. Cool.

3. Beat eggs, sugar, vanilla, lemon juice and zest together. Add melted butter, toasted coconut and dried cherries. Sift together ⅓ cup flour and baking powder. Stir into mixture.

4. Pour over baked crust. Bake for 25 minutes.

5. While bars are still warm dust with additional powdered sugar. Cool and cut into bars.

343

Logging, circa 1955
Jim Parsons Jr. Collection

Autumn Glory, Sand Creek
Brendan Rodgers

Restaurants

John Selle Dining Room in the Charles Selle Logging Camp about 1905. Bonner County Historical Socierty Collection

Homemade Baked Manicotti
Arlo's Ristoranté

1	lb. fresh Ricotta cheese
4	oz. Parmesan cheese, grated
4	oz. provolone cheese, diced
2	tbsp. fresh Italian Parsley, chopped
1	egg
4	pasta sheets
	salt and pepper to taste
2	cups Marinara sauce

Preheat oven to 350°.

1. Combine 3 cheeses, parsley, egg, salt and pepper.

2. Divide cheese mixture evenly between 4 pasta sheets, spreading along one edge of sheet and roll.

3. Spread ½ cup Marinara sauce in bottom of an 8" x 9" x 2" pan. Place Manicotti in baking dish and top with 1½ cups Marinara.

4. Bake for 20 minutes and serve.

Wild Mushroom Risotto

Beyond Hope Restaurant

2	tbsp. fresh minced shallots
2	tbsp. fresh minced garlic
4	tbsp. clarified butter
1	cup white wine
2	cups Arborio rice
2	oz. morel mushrooms rehydrated in 5 cups hot water and 2 tbsp. mushroom base
1½	cups heavy cream
2	oz. shredded Fontina cheese
4	oz. sliced crimini mushrooms

1. Sauté shallots and garlic in butter until translucent, but not browned.

2. Deglaze pan with white wine and reduce by half.

3. Add rice, stirring constantly until liquid is absorbed.

4. Remove morels from hot water and add liquid ¼ cup at a time to rice. Be sure that at the end of this process you do not pour dirt from bottom of container into rice. Utilize all of liquid. Stir constantly.

5. Add cream, stirring constantly, until ¾ absorbed. Add cheese, mushrooms and continue stirring until cheese melts.

6. Serve immediately. Serves six. We like to use local morels that we dry in the spring.

349

Stuffed Double Pork Chops

Beyond Hope Restaurant

4   cloves roasted garlic
6   oz. goat cheese
3   tbsp. fresh chiffonade basil
2   tbsp. sun dried tomatoes
6   12 oz. pork chops (thick cut, Frenched)
5   tbsp. olive oil
      salt and pepper to taste
      dry wine
      butter

Preheat oven to 450°.

1. In small bowl smash garlic with fork. Add goat cheese, basil and sun dried tomatoes and mix well.

2. On back of pork chop use a paring knife to cut hole. Slide blade into center of chop. Keep butt of knife stationary. Do not widen opening; just rock knife back and forth inside chop to create a pocket.

3. Stuff each chop with a tablespoon of cheese mixture.

4. Heat olive oil in skillet over medium high heat. Season chops with salt and pepper and place them in pan. Sear each side until browned.

5. Place in oven for about 20 minutes or until internal temperature is 145°. Remove chops from pan. Pour off oil.

6. Deglaze pan with wine. Add some butter to make a sauce and serve.

Left Amy Nettleingham and Friends, circa 1918.
Robert Gunter Collection

Pecan Chicken Salad with Goat Cheese, Pickled Red Onions & Apple Cider Vinaigrette

Café Trinity

Chef Gabriel Cruz

Pecan Chicken Breasts

2	5 oz. boneless, skinless chicken breasts pounded thin
1	cup ground pecans (medium ground)
	kosher salt
	fresh ground pepper
½	cup flour
2	beaten eggs
3	tbsp. canola oil
1	tbsp. butter

Pickled Red Onions

1	large red onion, julienne
1½	cups red wine vinegar
5	black pepper corns
½	cup honey
1	bay leaf

Apple Cider Vinaigrette

¼	cup apple cider vinegar
½	tsp. minced garlic
1	tbsp. minced shallots
	kosher salt and fresh ground pepper
¾	cup pure olive oil

Salad Base

2   handfuls mixed baby greens
½   cup goat cheese

Preheat oven to 375°.

1. To prepare the **Pecan Chicken Breast** heat oven-proof saute´ pan to medium heat. While heating pan, season breasts with salt and pepper. Dredge in flour and then the egg; finally pack pecans on the chicken breast.

2. When pan is hot, add oil and butter until it shimmers and then add the chicken breasts.

3. Brown on one side, turn and place in oven to bake for about 5 to 7 minutes or until done.

4. To prepare the **Pickled Red Onions** place vinegar, pepper corns, honey, bay leaf in a stainless steel pot. Bring to a boil; reduce heat and simmer for 5 minutes.

5. Place the red onions in a stainless steel bowl. Once the vinegar is ready strain it over the onions to remove the bay and the pepper corns. This can be prepared one day ahead, but no later than 3 hours before serving.

6. To prepare the **Apple Cider Vinaigrette,** whisk together the cider vinegar, garlic, shallots, salt and pepper in a stainless steel bowl.

7. Slowly whisk in the oil to emulsify vinegar and oil. Store until ready to use.

8. Just before serving add mixed greens to a large bowl; season with salt and pepper to taste. Drizzle Apple Cider Vinaigrette to taste and toss. Arrange on plate; sprinkle goat cheese around greens. Slice chicken breast diagonially; arrange on top of salad. Top with pickled red onions and serve.

Salsa Fresca

Chimney Rock Grill at Schweitzer Mountain Resort
Chef Michael Williams

5-10	tomatoes, diced
1	small red onion, diced
1	medium cucumber, diced
3	jalapeño peppers, diced
½	bunch cilantro, chopped
1	tbsp. cumin
1	tbsp. brown sugar
1	tbsp. red wine vinegar
½	tsp. coriander
	cayenne to taste
	juice from one lemon
	juice from one lime
	salt and pepper to taste

Combine all ingredients and let stand one hour.

Guacamole

Chimney Rock Grill at Schweitzer Mountain Resort
Chef Michael Williams

3	cloves garlic
1	small white onion
¼	bunch cilantro
1-2	jalapeño peppers, stem removed
3-4	small tomatillos or regular tomatoes
3	large avocados (reserve the pits)
	a squeeze of lime juice
1	tbsp. kosher salt

1. Pureé garlic and white onion; pureé jalapeños, tomatillos and cilantro. Leave mixture slightly chunky. Combine pureés.

2. Peel and pit avocados. Add avocado halves and salt to pureés. Mash with a potato masher until chunky.

3. Add avocado pits back in and cover with plastic wrap.

4. Refrigerate for one hour.

Fish Taco Sauce

Chimney Rock Grill at Schweitzer Mountain Resort
Chef Michael Williams

1	minced jalapeño pepper
½	cup yogurt
½	cup mayonnaise
1	tsp. capers
1	tsp. fresh oregano
½	tsp. cumin
½	tsp. dill
¼	tsp. cayenne
	juice from one lime
	salt and pepper to taste

Mix all ingredients and let sit for one day.

Margarita Shrimp

Hill's Resort, Priest Lake
www.hillsresort.com

10	large peeled and deveined shrimp
4	oz. Margarita mix (recipe follows)
½	ripe avocado cut into small cubes
2	oz. whipping cream
2-3	oz. butter

Rice

1½	cups cooked rice
1	tsp. chicken base
1	tsp. rosemary

Margarita Mix

2	oz. tequila
1	oz. triple sec
1	oz. Rose's lime juice

1. Mix margarita mix ingredients together and set aside.

2. Add chicken base and rosemary to rice and keep warm.

3. Heat butter in large sauté pan and bring to medium heat.

3. Add shrimp and sauté until done (about 2 minutes).

4. Add margarita mix, diced avocado and cream.

5. Continue cooking until shrimp are done and sauce thickens slightly, about one minute. Stir occasionally.

Serve on a bed of rice. Serves two.

Huckleberry Pie

Hill's Resort, Priest Lake
www.hillsresort.com

1	9" baked pastry shell
4	cups washed huckleberries
¾	cup water
3	tbsp. cornstarch
1	cup sugar
1-3	tsp. fresh lemon juice
	whipped cream or ice cream

1. Simmer 1 cup of huckleberries with water for 3 to 4 minutes.

2. Combine cornstarch and sugar and add to cooking fruit.

3. Simmer slowly until syrup is thick and clear.

4. When thickened add lemon juice to taste; depending on berries' sweetness. Cool slightly.

5. Line pastry shell with 3 cups of berries, pour slightly cooled glaze over raw berries.

6. Mix gently with fork to coat fresh berries.

7. Chill thoroughly. Serve with whipped cream or ice cream.

Serves eight.

Barbecued Baby Back Ribs
Hill's Resort, Priest Lake

5	lb. baby back rib of pork (not cut up)
½	cup Burgundy wine
2	tbsp. liquid smoke
½	cup sliced white onions
2	stalks celery, chopped
1	tbsp. salt
½	tsp. pepper

Barbecue Sauce

4	cups catsup
2	tbsp. liquid smoke
½	cup brown sugar
2	tbsp. honey
½	cup broth, reserved from cooking ribs

1. Place ribs in a heavy pan; add water to cover. Add wine, liquid smoke, onion, celery, salt and pepper.

2. Bring to boil then simmer for one hour or until ribs are tender.

3. Cool in broth reserving ½ cup for later use. May be done a day before and refrigerated over night

4. Combine the sauce ingredients in 2 quart pan. Cook and stir over medium heat until mixture boils. Reduce heat and simmer 20 minutes. Stir occasionally.

5. Brown ribs under broiler or over charcoal grill. Turn occasionally. Baste with BBQ sauce for the last few minutes. Serve with additional sauce. Serves 5.

Huckleberry Daiquiri

Hill's Resort, Priest Lake
www.hillsresort.com

1¼	oz. white rum
¼	cup huckleberries
1	tbsp. simple syrup (½ water, ½ cup sugar)
1½	cups ice
¼	cup orange juice

1. Blend all ingredients in blender until smooth.

2. Serve in a tall glass and garnish with orange slice and cherry.

Serves one.

Sugo Contadina

Ivano's Ristoranté and Cafe

6	oz. Italian sausage
¼	cup plus 3 tbsp. extra virgin olive oil
2	tbsp. chopped garlic
2	oz. white wine
2	cups Ivano's Pomodoro sauce
	pinch red chili flakes
2	oz. heavy cream
½	lb. rigatoni, cook before adding to sauce
	fresh grated Parmesan cheese

1. Brown sausage in ¼ cup olive oil, pour off grease and put sausage aside.

2. Add 3 tbsp. olive oil and garlic; cook until brown.

3. Add back sausage; add white wine, Pomodoro sauce, chili flakes and bring to boil.

4. Add cream; cook until reduced.

5. Toss into cooked pasta, top with fresh grated Parmesan cheese.

Wild Mushroom Cannelloni
with Three Cheese Sauce
The Floating Restaurant, Hope
www.hopefloatingrestaurant.com

16	tubes of cannelloni
2	cups marinara sauce

Wild Mushroom Filling

1	lb. white mushrooms, sliced
2	lbs. forest mushrooms, sliced. You may use fresh shitakes, portabellas, criminis and morels
1	medium onion, small dice
2	tbsp. garlic, chopped
3	tbsp. butter
1	tsp. dried tarragon
1	tsp. dried basil
½	cup brandy
½	cup white wine
1	cup heavy cream
	salt and pepper to taste

Three Cheese Cream Sauce

1	cup half and half
1	tbsp. roux or other thickening agent
2	tbsp. shredded Parmesan
2	oz. shredded Provolone or Swiss
1	oz. blue cheese
1	cup whipping cream
	salt and pepper to taste

362

Preheat oven to 350°.

1. Sauté chopped onion, garlic and all sliced mushrooms in butter. Add dry herbs, brandy, wine and cream.

2. Turn to low heat and simmer until all liquid is absorbed. Stir occasionally towards end to prevent burning. Finish with salt and pepper to taste. Cool.

3. Make roux for sauce by melting 2 tbsp. butter, adding 2 tbsp. flour and stirring until smooth and lightly browned.

4. For sauce, add 1 tbsp. roux to half and half and heat to simmer, stirring constantly until thickened. Gradually stir in all 3 cheeses.

5. In a large saucepan, heat cream to scalding. Add thickened cheese sauce. Continue simmering over low heat for 20 minutes. Salt and pepper to taste.

6. To assemble cannelloni, fill tubes with cooled mushroom filling.

7. Pour marinara into a baking dish and line up filled tubes over the marinara.

8. Cover with foil and bake for about 25 minutes. Remove and drizzle with hot cream sauce.

Makes 16 tubes. Can be frozen.

Thai Summer Duck

Sand Creek Grill

4   cups linguine, boiled
8   duck breasts
       salt and pepper to taste

Preheat oven to 425°.

1. Heat oil in large skillet until almost smoking.

2. Season duck breasts with salt and pepper. Sear skin side down until brown and cripsy.

3. Flip duck and place in oven to finish cooking about 6 to 8 minutes.

4. While duck is in the oven, heat another large pan with olive oil.

5. Add linguine and a little white cooking wine to steam linguine. Remove from stove and toss with Spicy Peanut Dressing to coat, page 365.

6. Remove duck from oven and slice on bias (across grain).

7. Serve over Peanut Noodles with Daikon Slaw, page 366.

Spicy Peanut Dressing
Sand Creek Grill

2	cups smooth peanut butter
1	cup freshly brewed black tea
1	cup orange juice
6	tbsp. sesame oil
6	tbsp. honey
4	tbsp. soy sauce
4	tbsp. rice vinegar
2	tbsp. minced ginger
4	tsp. grated orange peel
6	cloves garlic
1½	tsp. chipotle powder

1. Blend all ingredients in blender.

2. Store

Daikon Slaw
Sand Creek Grill

2	cups Daikon, cut into long matchsticks
1	cup chopped green onion
2	cucumbers, cut into long matchsticks
1	cup red cabbage, fine chiffonade
½	cup fresh mint, chopped
½	cup cilantro, chopped

Add Daikon Dressing and mix in bowl.

Daikon Dressing

½	cup lemon juice
¼	cup sugar

In a small saucepan boil to make a simple syrup.

1	cup rice wine vinegar
½	cup olive oil
	fresh ground pepper to taste

Add the simple syrup, rice wine vinegar, olive oil and fresh ground pepper in a blender. Blend well.

Slaw and dressing can be refrigerated for up to 1 day.

COMMUNITY ASSISTANCE LEAGUE

est. 1979 Sandpoint Idaho

July 4, 2003
Rodger Branscome

Community Assistance League

Dynamic volunteers helping our community

Mission Statement

Community Assistance League of Sandpoint supports our community through education, service and philanthropy.

Grants for 2006 totalled $25,000

CAL Scholarships, 2006

15 Scholarships totalling $13,350

Kaleidoscope Children's Art Program
Sandpoint Tennis Association
Hope-Clark Fork Chamber of Commerce
Bonner County Homeless Task Force
Sandpoint Parks and Recreation
Blanchard Area Seniors
Memorial Community Center at Hope
Bonner County Humane Society
Clark Fork-Hope Senior Center
Asphalt Angels Car Club of Priest River
Tri-State Water Council
Bonner Community Food Center
Panhandle Animal Shelter
Pend Oreille Arts Council *Ovations* Program
Pend Oreille Arts Council *Perspectives* Program
Priest River Chamber of Commerce
Bonner Community Hospice
Calvary Chapel Livewire Youth Center
Friends of the West Bonner County Library
Bonner Partners in Care Clinic
Clark Fork Valley Fire Department
Farmin Stidwell PTA
Panhandle Special Needs
Sandpoint TEEN Council
Sandpoint Senior Center

CAL was organized in 1979 with 16 members and now its membership is near 200.

Extreme Makeover, 2005

Bizarre Bazaar-Upscale Resale

Helen Williams-Baker, President

2006 Board

Past Presidents

CAL Activities

Enchilada Sale

Kaleidoscope
Kathy Borders & Deb Lafrenz

Blankie Program

Bizarre Bazaar Sale, 2005

Acknowledgements

Photography Credits

Bond-Bowie, Carol and Bond, Diana, Collection.
Bonner County Daily Bee, Photographer Roger Branscome.
Bonner County Historical Society Collection.
Burt, Mae and Walter, Family Collection.
Cline, Foster, MD., Photographer.
Gunter, Robert, Historian and Writer.
Hall, Dann, Professional Photographer.
Kirking, Dagmar and Marvin, Family Collection.
Mock, Jay, Professional Photographer.
Park, Frederick, Cover photograph of Gold Hill.
Parsons, Clarice and Jim Jr. Family Collection.
Rodgers, Brendan, Landscape Photographer.
Scotchman Peak, Hough, Philip, Photographer.

Data Input

Patty Bowman
Janae Dale
Catherine Deacon
Mary Jo Haag
Jan Morgenstern

Jan McKeogh
Evelyn Meany
Polly Mire
Nancy Hahn Rodgers

Recipe Testers & Contributors

The Community Assistance League gratefully acknowledges its members and families for the enormous commitment and contributions. They gave time and talent to select the best recipes chosen for their inspiring use of ingredients and their fresh approach to good taste. Thank you to all who have submitted your favorite recipes, helpful hints and cooking tips. We sincerely hope that we have not inadvertently omitted any contributor.

Acknowledgements

Judy Ahrend
Valerie Albi
Jacquie Albright
Mary Jo Ambrosiani
Joyce Anderson
Carolyn Apple
Eileen Atkisson
Barbara Balbi
Christina Baker
Grete Bame
Martha Bauer
Mary Bauer
Pamela Riddle Bird
Kathy Borders
Linda Both
Patty Bowman
Angela Brass
Sharon Brill
Joan Brittain
Irene Broderick
Sue Brooks
Sue Helen Brown
Suzy Bryant
Barbee Buchanan
Marjorie Butts
Mindy Cameron
Sandi Campbell
Diana Carlson
Barbara Carver, Rev.
Darcy Chambers
Cynthia Chenault
Hermie Cline
Vivian Congreve
Elise L. Creed
Janae Dale
Frances Davis
Diana L. Dawson
Katherine Deacon
Carol Deaner
Donna Dieffenbach
Betty Ann Diehl

Kim Diercks
Joyce Ann Dillon
Judy Fitzgerald-Dolan
Nandy Dunnagan
Gretchen Duykers
Barbara Eacret
Wendy Eacret
Jacqueline Earle
Teri Enger
Wendy Emmer
Sherry Ennis
Carroll Ensminger
Rose Escalante
Carol Fels
Joyce Fenton
Debbie Ferguson
Paula Fitzsimmons
Kathleen Flaherty
Phyllis Foro
Annette Fraser-Runnalls
Latimer Frazier
Sherry Fulton
Kathy Gavin
Joanne Gay
Kathy George
Tracy Gibson
Catherine Gilchrist
Sue Gillespie
Sonia Gladish
Lesley Goffinet
Carol Gollin
Jeannette Graham
Mary Jo Haag
Valarie Hallmark
Donna Hamblin
Betsy Harding
Linda Hart
Barb Hecker
Bette Heffner
Heather Hellier
Elizabeth Holden

Acknowledgements

Connie Horton
Arlene Howell
Lorri Huesers
Denise Huguenin
Sylvia Humes
Pamela Irwin
Deanna James
Carol Jenkins
Ginny Jensen
Barbara Jorgensen
Sammie Justesen
Marge Kamplain
Mona Kelly
Shawn Keough
Charie Kerr
Christine Kester
Linda Kirchmann
Vivian Kirkwood
Ilani Kopiecki
Charlene Krames
Robyn Kuhl
Bonnie Lackey
Deb Lafrenz
Judy Lange
Fran Lara
Sandra Lawrence
Gail Legget
Karry Lensing
Nancy Lewis
Pat Lewis
Sally Lindemann
Elaine Linscott
Kelli Locascio
Sally Lowry
Maribeth Lynch
Darleen Macek
Barbara MacIsaac
Liv Helene Mackay
Lois MacLeod-Kehoe
Sheryl MacMenami
Carolyn Marshall

Madeline McClelland
Marilynn McDonald
Melinda McDonald
Jan Mckeough
Evelyn Meany
Sherry Metz
Polly Mire
Susan Moore
"J" Morgan
Jan Morgenstern
Kathy Morris
Phyllis Morris
Linda Muskopf
Linda Nelson
Marcella Nelson
Linda Omundson
Rosemarie Osmunson
Patricia Otto
Marilyn Pagano
Carol Page
Terri Palmer
Sally Park
Shawna Parry
Clarice Parsons
Susan Peck
Anita Perry
Marcia Phillips
Lynn Piper
Pat Ramsey
Kelly Rasco
Patti Rechnitzer
Lisa Richards
Susie Richardson
Jane Ingram Riter
Nancy Hahn Rodgers
Ann Roen
Janet Rogers
Bernice Rosenthal
Madelen Rowe
Marilyn Sabella
Barb Shaw

Acknowledgements

Bev Shaw
Darlene Shelly
Jeanelle Shields
Tawnie Sleep
Wilma Smith
Annette Smuin
Sally Sonnichsen
Joyce Spiller
Dixie Stansell
Joy Stevens
Patricia Stevens
Susie Summerhill
Marguerite Suttmeier
Jan Swales
Helen Tapp
Carol Thomas
Helen Thompson
RoseMarie Thompson
Judy Thompson
Shirley Thornton
Mary Ann Tomt
Marie Valentine
Sydne VanHorne
Paula Vinton
Sue Vogelsinger
J'nene Wade
Ellie Walterscheidt
Joan Wanamaker
Miriam Weiss
Barbara Wilcox
Viva J. Wiley
Helen Williams-Baker
Marsha Williams
Wanita Willinger
Marcia Wilson
Tere Wilson
Carolyn Winkelmann
Nancy Wood
Melanie Young

373

Index

N

O

P

Y

Z

"Rolling On"
Jim Parsons Jr. Collection

Mail Order Form

Community Assistance League
PO Box 1361
Sandpoint, ID 8386
208.263.3400

Price   Quantity   Total
$25.00 _____   _____   _____

Shipping & handling $5.00
per book.   _____

Name_____   Please charge my Visa___ Mastercard___

Address_____   Account #_____

Telephone _____   Expiration Date_____ _____

                                   Signature _____

Please make checks out to Community Assistance League.
Please do not send cash.
Photocopies of mail order form accepted.   383